Digital Dharma

Digital Dharma

Finding Stillness in an Age of Screens

Fatima al-Karim

Mindful Pages

Published in 2026

ISBN: 9789374121559 (PB)
ISBN: 9789374122389 (eBook)

Published by

Mindful Pages
Imprint of Alpha Editions LLC
312 W. 2nd St #1834
Casper, WY 82601, USA

This book was developed using advanced writing tools to support the drafting and ideation process. All content has been thoughtfully curated, refined, and reviewed to ensure quality and relevance.

Content

Introduction
Digital Dharma – Finding Stillness in an Age of Screens

The last time you checked your phone, did you choose to, or did something in you simply move before your mind caught up? The gesture feels trivial—a twitch of the thumb, a flick of the wrist—but it is, in miniature, a map of the modern condition. We no longer reach for the device as much as it reaches through us. The screen hums, not just with information but with invitation. It promises relevance, connection, stimulation—yet leaves a residue of restlessness that lingers long after the battery dies.

Once, a monk told a product manager that the problem wasn't the phone but the reflex that reached for it. The monk, schooled in the anatomy of attention, recognised in that reflex an ancient rhythm—craving, grasping, brief relief—dressed in glass and algorithms. The manager, a connoisseur of engagement metrics, understood that same reflex as a feature, not a flaw. Between these two worldviews—one contemplative, one commercial—lies the central tension of our time: how to live sanely amid tools that have learned to pull the mind's strings.

This book begins from a simple, radical premise: enlightenment is incompatible with compulsion, not with connectivity. The digital world, far from being an obstacle to stillness, can become its training ground—if we learn to inhabit it differently. Our devices are not enemies of attention but mirrors of it; what they reflect back is the quality of our own awareness. The true challenge, then, is not to escape technology, but to reimagine our relationship with it—to turn each notification into a bell of mindfulness rather than a summons to distraction.

The promise of *Digital Dharma* is neither abstinence nor alarmism. It is a manual for moral and cognitive design—a way of using the very systems that seduce us as laboratories for self-mastery. Here, attention becomes a moral act, detachment a design choice, and stillness a repeatable protocol.

In the early decades of the twenty-first century, the attention economy became the world's most lucrative religion. Its creed was simple: keep them watching. The world's largest corporations found their altar in the pocket and their scripture in the scroll. Every click, every pause, every micro-expression fed an invisible calculus of engagement. Yet beneath the convenience, another economy thrived—an exchange of autonomy for ease, of time for trivia, of agency for algorithmic suggestion.

To understand the stakes, consider this: the average person touches their phone over two thousand times a day. That number, while staggering, is less significant than the pattern it represents—a perpetual oscillation between boredom and relief, anxiety and affirmation. What looks like use is often being used; what feels like choice is frequently choreography. The modern interface is not neutral. It is a behavioural environment, engineered to capture and monetise attention.

But moralising against technology misses the deeper issue. The craving that drives us to check our feeds is not new. The Buddha called it *tanha*—thirst. The Stoics called it attachment to externals. The mystics called it forgetting. The screens merely give ancient habit loops a glossy finish. To scold the device is to mistake the mirror for the face.

This book does not call for withdrawal but for wakefulness. We will treat our tools as teachers, not tempters. Through the lenses of cognitive science, design ethics, and contemplative practice, we will examine how technologies sculpt our minds—and how, through deliberate redesign, those same tools can cultivate the virtues they currently erode.

Consider the paradox: never in history have humans been so connected, yet never have they felt so dispersed. We communicate across oceans instantly but struggle to sustain attention across sentences. We multitask to the point of absurdity, mistaking busyness for meaning. The ancient injunction to "remember yourself" now requires literal software.

Our predicament is not technological but spiritual. Each new notification confronts us with a moral question: will we be driven, or will we choose? In an age that prizes immediacy, stillness becomes rebellion. To pause before responding—to breathe before scrolling—is to reclaim a fragment of sovereignty. It is to practise freedom at the speed of habit.

This is what I call *digital dharma*: the alignment of intention and action under conditions of distraction. The word *dharma* here is not a call to creed but to coherence. It refers to that which holds—the lawful relationship between inner states and outer acts. Applied to the digital world, it asks: does this technology help me remember who I am, or does it help me forget?

Digital Dharma is built on four disciplines, woven through its chapters: attention, design, ethics, and embodiment. Each discipline translates a timeless virtue into a modern skill. Attention trains the mind to return. Design reframes tools as moral architecture. Ethics guides speech and interaction in the accelerated spaces of the web. Embodiment grounds stillness not in theory but in breath, posture, and presence. Together, they form a living system for digital sanity.

We begin in Chapter One, *The Monk and the Metrics*, where attention is reclaimed from its corporate captivity. We will dismantle the myths of "focus" and "productivity" and reveal attention as a dynamic act of remembrance—the ability to return to what matters. You will learn to see through the business models that profit from distraction, to distinguish convenience from coercion, and to define your own digital dharma.

In Chapter Two, *The Loop and the Bell*, we turn from analysis to experiment. You will map your own habit loops, those tiny rituals of reach and reward that govern more of your life than you realise. We will then design counter-rituals—micro-fasts, mindful notifications, and intentional interruptions—that turn your environment into an ally rather than an adversary.

By Chapter Three, *Ethics at the Speed of Send*, the lens widens. The ethics of speech and reaction—ancient preoccupations of monks and philosophers—reappear in the age of instant communication.

How do we speak truthfully and beneficially when our words travel faster than our reflection? What does compassion look like in a comment thread?

Chapter Four, *The Body Remembers the Feed*, grounds the inquiry in physiology. The feed does not only capture the mind; it inhabits the body—through breath patterns, eye movements, muscle tension. Here you will learn somatic techniques for rebalancing attention, reprogramming rest, and restoring the body's role as the foundation of mindfulness.

By Chapter Five, *Tools That Tell the Truth*, theory meets architecture. We will explore humane design—how friction can serve virtue, how metrics can measure meaning, and how to build personal charters that translate ethics into operation. This is not self-help but self-governance: the deliberate shaping of one's digital habitat.

The next chapters widen the frame from individual to collective. In *Community as an Antidote*, we see that shared protocols outlast private willpower. Attention is contagious; so is integrity. We will study how households, teams, and schools can institutionalise mindful norms without lapsing into dogma or moral posturing.

Work Without Whiplash turns the lens on professional life. Here the question becomes practical: how can we design workflows, meetings, and communications that honour cognitive limits? Stillness is not a luxury for monks; it is a prerequisite for sound judgement in a world of permanent urgency.

Finally, *The Stillness Protocol* distils the book's philosophy into a framework: Attention → Intention → Design → Practice. You will learn how to diagnose distractions, run humane interventions, and sustain change through a living charter that evolves with your life.

The book closes, fittingly, not with mastery but mercy. *Grace After the Feed* argues that compassion is the final skill—towards others, yes, but above all towards oneself. The path of digital dharma is not linear progress but cyclical remembering. We fail, we return, we continue. That rhythm is the practice.

What, then, is at stake? In a word: agency. Every flick, swipe, and scroll rewrites the nervous system. The question is no longer whether technology changes us—it has—but whether we can shape that change consciously. The same neural plasticity that makes us manipulable also makes us trainable. The same algorithms that exploit our impulses can be used to reveal them. The tools that fragment our attention can, paradoxically, teach us how to hold it.

Our species has always built mirrors—polished stone, silver glass, glowing pixels. Each era believes its reflection unique. Yet the mirror has never been the problem. What we fear is what we see within it: a mind that cannot sit still. This book is a long meditation on that image and a practical invitation to transform it.

Imagine, for a moment, that your phone were not a portal of distraction but a partner in awareness; that every buzz were a bell reminding you to return; that every screen became a surface for discipline, not desire. This is not fantasy but training. It begins not by renouncing the world but by reinhabiting it—with precision, with grace, and with deliberate stillness.

So before we proceed, pause. Feel the device in your hand. The weight, the texture, the hum. This is not your enemy. It is your mirror. What you do next—this very next breath, this next touch—will decide whether it governs you, or you govern it.

Welcome to *Digital Dharma.*

Chapter 1
The Monk and the Metrics

In 2016, a Silicon Valley engineer sat in a silent monastery in the hills of Northern Thailand, fidgeting with a mala bead between his fingers as if it were a touchscreen. He had built software designed to "maximise engagement," yet after three days of meditation, he could barely sit still for ten minutes. His teacher, a thin monk with an expression of unbothered clarity, finally leaned towards him and said, "You see? You did not invent distraction. You only gave it better fonts." The line landed like a koan—dry, humorous, precise. What the engineer realised in that moment, and what this chapter will make explicit, is that the modern crisis of attention is not a new disease but a perfected design.

Every civilisation has had its way of scattering the mind. The difference is that ours has found a way to monetise it. The device in your hand is not only a tool of communication; it is the world's most efficient slot machine. Each swipe, each scroll, each refresh carries the faint promise of reward—a message, a like, a flash of novelty—and, beneath it, the echo of the same neural machinery that once kept our ancestors scanning the savannah for fruit or threat. We are, in other words, ancient minds running on modern hardware. The product managers know this. The monks have always known this.

Attention, that invisible currency of consciousness, is being traded at scale. The platforms call it engagement; the advertisers call it reach; the users call it connection. But what it really measures is surrender—the gradual outsourcing of agency to systems optimised not for our flourishing but for our fixation. The metrics may be digital, but the loss is existential. What we attend to becomes who we are; what we are distracted by becomes what we forget to become.

And yet, attention is not merely a faculty to protect—it is a practice to cultivate. To attend is not simply to focus, as one might focus a camera lens. It is to choose, moment by moment, what will enter consciousness and what will not. It is the mind's steering wheel, the invisible hinge between perception and action. The tragedy of the digital age is not that our attention is weak but that it is misdirected, continuously hijacked by designs that treat every moment of boredom as a revenue opportunity.

This chapter begins by dismantling the myth that attention is a finite resource to be hoarded. It is, rather, a skill—selective control over perception and action, refined through remembering and returning. Cognitive science gives us the scaffolding: working memory's fragile bandwidth, the neural economics of reward prediction, the dopamine drip of uncertain outcomes. Buddhist psychology provides the vocabulary: *sati*, the discipline of remembering to remember. When fused, these perspectives transform attention from a state one possesses to a verb one practises. The question shifts from *How long can I focus?* to *How swiftly can I return?*

The monk and the metric meet here. Where engineers speak of retention curves, the contemplative speaks of returning. The technology of attention has always existed—it is called awareness—but in the digital age, it requires a firmware update. The challenge is not to eliminate stimuli but to learn how to navigate them with discernment. This, in essence, is the first lesson of digital dharma: the problem is not connectivity; it is compulsion.

To grasp why this matters, we must understand the business model of distraction. The attention economy, beneath its glamour of innovation, is an elaborate form of behavioural capture. Every "free" service you use is a contract written in invisible ink. The price is not money but bandwidth—the finite cycles of thought and feeling that could have gone elsewhere. Behind every feed lies a machinery of surveillance: eye-tracking data, emotional inference, predictive analytics. The goal is not to show you what you want but to train you to want what you're shown.

And yet, moral outrage alone is too easy. Outrage feels righteous but solves nothing. The more intelligent stance is design literacy: to see not just manipulation but the incentive structures that make it inevitable. Platforms optimise for engagement because their survival depends on it. Once we understand that, we can stop moralising and start intervening—designing our environments as carefully as the platforms design theirs. The point is not to vilify technology but to reclaim authorship of its use.

Here we encounter a more subtle corruption: convenience. It arrives as kindness, then quietly erodes choice. A one-click purchase saves a few seconds; an autoplay saves you the decision to stop. But after enough iterations, ease turns into inertia. The friction that once protected reflection is sanded away, and what remains is pure stimulus-response—a behavioural reflex wrapped in luxury UX. We call it seamless; the truth is, we've lost the seams that once gave shape to experience.

This chapter offers a simple diagnostic: does a feature reduce friction or remove freedom? The difference marks the boundary between usability and coercion. Every designer must confront it. Every user must learn to sense it. To live ethically with technology is to know when a convenience has become a cage.

From this exploration emerges a working definition of *digital dharma.* In Sanskrit, *dharma* means that which holds—lawfulness, alignment, integrity. To act in accordance with dharma is to bring intention and action into harmony, even amidst noise. Translated for the digital context, it asks: do my tools help me live in alignment with my values, or do they scatter me away from them? This is not asceticism; it is calibration. Non-harm becomes mindful consumption. Right effort becomes sustainable focus. Right speech becomes clarity in a message thread.

If attention is the raw material of consciousness, then dharma is its architecture—the way in which awareness takes ethical shape. The first step in reclaiming that architecture is diagnosis: to see the loops we are caught in, to trace the metrics that shape our days, to name the coercions disguised as kindness. The next step is design: to build habits, tools, and boundaries that turn awareness into agency.

Throughout this chapter, you will learn to see your environment as both a mirror and a training ground. You will dissect the habit loops encoded in apps, the reward systems that keep you scrolling, the persuasive architectures that trade your intention for their metrics. You will also learn how to subvert them—not through withdrawal, but through redesign. Each device becomes a dojo; each notification, a bell.

We are accustomed to thinking of enlightenment as an escape from the world's noise. This chapter proposes the opposite: that enlightenment begins in the midst of it, as a precise and deliberate relationship to attention. Stillness, in this view, is not the absence of stimuli but the mastery of response. The monk knew it long before the metrics existed. The engineer learned it too late. You, the reader, are in a position to learn it now—before the reflex becomes the self.

By the time you finish this chapter, you will see attention not as a resource to protect but as a moral technology to refine. You will have a framework for evaluating tools by their ability to support your returns rather than deepen your grips. And, most importantly, you will begin to sense that every act of awareness—every mindful return—is an act of quiet rebellion against an economy built on your distraction.

The screens are not going away. But neither is your capacity for deliberate stillness. This is where the monk meets the metric—not in opposition, but in synthesis. The metric measures behaviour; the monk observes it. Between them lies your freedom.

What Attention Actually Is

In September 2010, at the University of Oxford's Department of Experimental Psychology, Professor Kia Nobre and her team published a study showing that human attention flickers rhythmically, like a lighthouse beam, roughly four times per second. The discovery unsettled a century of assumptions. Attention, long imagined as a steady spotlight, turned out to be a pulse—a dynamic pattern of sampling and selection. What you "focus" on is not continuously illuminated but revisited again and again, refreshed by cycles of choice. The mind, it seems, is never still; it is a disciplined oscillation. This rhythm, Nobre noted, is both limitation and opportunity: it exposes why distraction is so easy—and why return is always possible.

Most people confuse attention with concentration, as though both were synonyms for effort. But attention is not the act of furrowing the brow or grinding through tasks. It is, rather, the selective control of perception and action. Each second, your senses bombard you with more data than your brain could ever process. To function at all, you must filter ruthlessly. That filtering—deciding what enters awareness and what is ignored—is attention. It is not an emotion, not a virtue, but an allocation system, the mind's internal economics. And, like any economy, it is governed by scarcity.

Neuroscientists estimate that working memory can hold between four and seven discrete chunks of information at once (Cowan, 2010). That limitation shapes everything from why we forget names at parties to why multitasking is largely fiction. Try reading an email while composing another, and you will feel the bottleneck: the brain is not doing both simultaneously but switching—costly, rapid toggling that drains energy and increases error. The problem is not moral weakness; it is architecture. Every act of divided attention exacts a toll in time and accuracy, as measurable as money leaving an account.

Yet scarcity alone does not explain why our devices exert such power. For that, one must look to *reward prediction error*—the brain's mechanism for learning from uncertainty. When an expected reward arrives (a message, a like, a ping), dopamine levels stabilise; but when the reward is uncertain, they spike. This principle, identified by Wolfram Schultz at Cambridge in 1997, is the same one that drives slot machines and stock trading. Variable outcomes maximise engagement because they turn curiosity into craving. The endless scroll, the notification badge, the "pull to refresh"—these are not arbitrary design flourishes but embodiments of a precise neuropsychological insight: uncertainty keeps you checking.

In this sense, the feed is not just content—it is choreography. Each platform trains your mind in a rhythm of anticipation and relief, repetition and return. It rewards the act of reaching more than the act of reading. Over time, this pattern rewires expectation itself: the user learns to seek stimulation not for its substance but for its timing. The attention economy thus transforms awareness into a conditioned reflex. To reclaim it requires understanding not only how attention is stolen but how it works when it is free.

Centuries before dopamine was named, Buddhist psychology mapped this same terrain with different tools. In the *Satipaṭṭhāna Sutta*—the foundational discourse on mindfulness, dated roughly to the 1st century BCE—attention (*sati*) is described not as concentration but as remembrance: the capacity to return, to recall one's purpose in the instant it is forgotten. To be attentive is to remember what one is doing while one is doing it. The meditative instruction "return to the breath" is not a reprimand for wandering but a rehearsal of this remembering. Each return strengthens the capacity to notice; each noticing refines the ability to return.

This ancient framing has striking resonance with modern cognitive models. Where psychology speaks of working memory updating, *sati* speaks of the interval between forgetting and remembering. Where behavioural science describes feedback loops, Buddhism describes samsara—the wheel of reactivity that can be interrupted only through awareness. The wisdom is the same: attention is not a static condition but a cycle, and mastery lies not in never lapsing but in noticing faster.

This redefinition matters, because it changes how we evaluate our tools. Most technologies today are judged by grip—how long they can hold your gaze, how "sticky" their design. But if attention is a practice of returning rather than staying, then the better metric is how easily a tool lets you step away and come back with intention. A well-designed app, in this light, is not one that enslaves focus but one that supports its rhythmic restoration. The question becomes moral: does this interface cultivate agency, or does it erode it?

Consider two examples. In 2015, the meditation app Headspace introduced a subtle design choice: when a session ends, the screen stays still. No autoplay, no suggestions, no dopamine bridge to the next thing. The experience ends cleanly, inviting pause. In contrast, YouTube's autoplay feature, launched in 2014, blurs endings entirely—each video melts into the next. The result is predictable: engagement soars, but autonomy decays. The difference between those two interfaces is not trivial; it is ethical. One reinforces the capacity to return; the other dissolves it.

A counterexample complicates the picture. In 2019, Apple introduced "Screen Time," a dashboard quantifying users' digital habits. The intent was virtuous—transparency, self-regulation. Yet for many, the feature became another site of anxiety, a daily guilt ritual rather than a guide. Data without compassion breeds self-punishment. The lesson: awareness must be paired with kindness; attention weaponised against the self is just another form of compulsion. The goal is not abstinence but alignment.

If attention is selective control, then control itself must be understood not as dominance but as design. The environments we inhabit—physical or digital—determine what is easy to notice and what is easy to forget. In a monastery, the bell cues returning. In a smartphone, the notification does. The question is who sets the cue, and for whose purpose. Technology can serve *sati* or sabotage it depending on whether its design invites choice or assumes consent.

One might test this principle in daily practice. Observe your device: how many of its features allow interruption by invitation rather than intrusion? Do you choose when to engage, or are you chosen? The distinction is subtle but profound. The ethical dimension of attention lies here—in the governance of entry and exit, in the rhythm of engagement. The path is neither withdrawal nor indulgence but calibration: learning to engineer your own returns.

Working memory, reward prediction, and *sati* all converge on one conclusion: awareness is a living loop. It depletes, refreshes, and refines itself through repetition. A distracted mind is not a failure but an untrained rhythm. Modern life, with its infinite stimuli, exaggerates this loop until it fractures. But it can also train it—if we learn to see every lapse not as loss but as opportunity for return.

In this respect, the metaphor of the pulse—first glimpsed in Nobre's 2010 experiment—becomes a motif worth keeping. Attention is not a fortress but a heartbeat. Each beat alternates between contraction and release, focus and renewal. The trick is not to make the heart stop beating, but to synchronise it with intention. Technology, when wisely designed, can align with that rhythm; when not, it accelerates it to exhaustion.

The implication reaches beyond personal productivity. In a world governed by metrics—click-through rates, dwell times, engagement minutes—the ability to attend deliberately becomes a form of resistance. Every act of returning undermines the calculus of capture. To attend freely is to refuse to be measured purely by retention.

And yet, the challenge remains unresolved. Can we build systems that measure not how long we stare, but how meaningfully we return? Could attention itself become the next frontier of ethical design—a discipline where success is defined by sovereignty, not stickiness? The answer, like attention itself, will depend on how quickly we remember what we were doing before we forgot.

The Business Model of Distraction

On 18 March 2018, *The Observer* published a story that jolted Silicon Valley's confidence in its own benevolence. The journalist Carole Cadwalladr revealed how Cambridge Analytica had harvested the Facebook data of over 87 million users to influence elections, including the 2016 US presidential race. The mechanics were technical; the principle was ancient. People were not persuaded by argument but by attention—what they looked at, what they lingered over, what they could not ignore. The scandal made explicit what technologists already knew but preferred not to say aloud: that human focus had become the raw material of a new industrial order.

The attention economy rests on a paradox so deep it feels invisible. The platforms that dominate modern communication—Facebook, YouTube, TikTok, X (formerly Twitter)—cost nothing to use yet command trillion-dollar valuations. The product, therefore, cannot be the service. The product is the user's cognitive bandwidth, auctioned in milliseconds to the highest bidder. Advertising has always traded on attention, but digital platforms transformed that trade into a continuous experiment, measuring and modulating human behaviour in real time. The result is not a marketplace of ideas but a marketplace of triggers.

To understand this model, we must start with its physics: data flow. Every click, pause, or scroll produces telemetry. That telemetry—timestamps, dwell times, cursor trajectories—is fed into algorithms trained to predict future engagement. Prediction begets manipulation. If an interface can anticipate what will keep you scrolling, it can design towards that outcome. This is not surveillance in the cinematic sense of spies and cameras, but a subtler form: surveillance as feedback loop. The system watches you to learn how to hold you.

Incentives sharpen the trap. Silicon Valley's dominant business model—advertising-supported free access—depends on a single key performance indicator: *time spent.* The longer you remain on a platform, the more data it collects and the more ads it serves. The user's attention becomes both means and end. Engineers are not paid to cultivate wellbeing; they are rewarded for engagement metrics. It is an elegant, amoral calculus. The design language that emerges—endless feeds, push notifications, autoplay—is not born of malice but of metric pressure. The machine optimises for what it measures.

Consider YouTube's "Up Next" algorithm, introduced in 2012. Researchers at Mozilla (2020) found that roughly 70 percent of total watch time on the platform is driven by algorithmic recommendations, not user choice. The recommendation engine learns which videos prolong viewing, often by nudging towards extremity—because outrage and novelty outperform calm or closure. The same principle governs the "For You" feed on TikTok, which by 2023 was consuming more aggregate user hours than Netflix. The success metric is not satisfaction but stickiness. The model rewards what captures, not what nourishes.

To label this manipulation is accurate but incomplete. The deeper dynamic is reinforcement learning—borrowed from behavioural psychology and rebranded as engagement optimisation. Variable-ratio reinforcement, first mapped by B. F. Skinner in 1957, describes how unpredictable rewards produce the strongest conditioning. Casinos rely on it; social media refined it. The refresh gesture on a phone mimics the lever pull of a slot machine. Sometimes you find something delightful, sometimes nothing. The uncertainty sustains the loop. Each update is a small wager of attention.

A counterexample clarifies the boundary. Wikipedia, founded in 2001, runs on a radically different model. Its pages are static, its revenue based on voluntary donations, its interface almost defiantly plain. The site's average visit length—around three minutes according to SimilarWeb (2023)—is a fraction of TikTok's average of 52 minutes per day. Yet Wikipedia's public trust levels remain among the highest of any digital platform. This contrast reveals a principle: when revenue is decoupled from retention, design incentives shift from capture to clarity. Attention ceases to be a currency and becomes a courtesy.

The business model of distraction thrives because it aligns profit with compulsion. Each user session is an experiment in nudging the next one. Data scientists call it *optimising for engagement*, but the behavioural outcome is indistinguishable from dependency. Still, condemnation alone misses the nuance. These systems are not merely addictive by design—they are adaptive by feedback. Their architects built machines that learn from human frailty faster than humans learn from the machines. The loops close silently.

For the user, the cost of "free" is not privacy alone but cognitive bandwidth. Each micro-interruption taxes working memory; each red badge dilutes context. The cumulative load is measurable. A 2019 University of Texas study found that even the presence of a smartphone—face down, powered off—reduced available cognitive capacity by up to 20 percent. The explanation is simple: vigilance consumes resources. The mind keeps part of itself tethered to the possibility of interruption. Attention, like power, bleeds away through standby mode.

To diagnose manipulation without resorting to moral panic, we must develop design literacy—a capacity to read interfaces as arguments. Every affordance carries an ethic. Infinite scroll, invented by Aza Raskin in 2006 at Humanized Ltd. in London, was intended to remove friction from information access. Raskin later called it "behavioural cocaine" for its ability to dissolve stopping cues. He did not design it to addict, but the metric incentives of downstream platforms converted a usability enhancement into a compulsion engine. Design, in other words, has no morality apart from the metrics it serves.

Surveillance data are not inherently evil; they are indifferent. Fitness trackers, for example, quantify movement to promote health. Yet even here, incentives distort outcomes. When the quantified self becomes the gamified self, attention shifts from experience to scorekeeping. The line between measurement and manipulation is crossed when data cease to inform and begin to incite. What makes the attention economy corrosive is not that it measures us, but that it measures us in units of distraction.

Critics often describe this ecosystem as exploitative, and rightly so, but exploitation is sustainable only because it feels rewarding. The interface flatters agency while quietly scripting it. We believe we are choosing; in reality, we are being choreographed. Still, the human response is not passive. People can and do resist. The rise of "focus modes" on iOS, the reintroduction of chronological feeds, and the emergence of minimalist phones such as the Light Phone II (2019, New York) signal a cultural countercurrent: design that respects withdrawal. Yet these remain niches within a system optimised for compulsion. The incentives are structural.

Here lies the unresolved dilemma: can an economy built on attention ever align with wellbeing? Advertising supports journalism, funds connectivity, and subsidises access for billions. To dismantle it entirely would be neither practical nor desirable. But to leave it unexamined is to accept a form of cognitive feudalism, where mental bandwidth is the rent we pay for convenience. Between moral panic and naïve optimism lies the harder path of redesign—changing metrics rather than merely moods.

Imagine if platforms measured *value created* rather than *time spent*; if success were defined by clarity, not captivity. The technology to do this exists. What is lacking is incentive. Investors do not fund contemplation; they fund growth curves. Users reward stimulation more readily than serenity. The algorithms follow our appetites. The business model of distraction, then, is not an alien imposition but a mirror.

The motif worth holding is the mirror. Every metric reflects a moral choice. We measure what we value, and by measuring it, we make it matter more. When engagement became the master metric, design followed suit. To reverse the trend, we must reassign moral weight to metrics that honour attention as a finite public good rather than an exploitable resource. That requires policy, design reform, and, above all, user discernment.

Yet no reform will erase the tension. The economics of attention and the ethics of awareness pull in opposite directions. The first seeks continuity; the second requires interruption. The question that remains, flickering like a notification just beyond reach, is deceptively simple: when the system rewards your distraction, what—if anything—will reward your return?

When Convenience Becomes Coercion

On 28 September 1999, in Seattle, the United States Patent and Trademark Office granted Amazon.com a patent for "1-Click" ordering. With a single press, customers could bypass the basket and purchase immediately. The outcome was concrete and commercial: fewer abandoned carts, smoother checkouts, faster revenue. A year later, in 2000, Apple licensed the patent in Cupertino to streamline its own online store. Ease became the business model. It also erased a seam—the small, deliberate pause when a user reviews a choice before committing. That seam had been a guardrail. Once gone, decisions accelerated beyond reflection.

The distinction between generosity and capture begins here. *Show*: one-click removes steps. *Name*: friction-lowering usability. *Explain*: usability reduces the cost of doing what a user already intends to do; it supports a decision that has formed. *Implication*: when a product removes steps *before* intention has stabilised, the same mechanism becomes a nudge toward action the user may not have chosen at a slower speed. The difference is moral, not merely technical. A seam can be a courtesy. It can also be a conscience.

Autoplay extends the logic. In 2014, YouTube, headquartered in San Bruno, introduced a default that queued the next video and began playback automatically. *Show*: endings blurred; the next clip started within seconds. *Name*: default-continuity design. *Explain*: by removing a stopping cue—your choice to click "play" again—the system shifts from service to script. Watch time rises because endings no longer feel like choices; they feel like inertia. *Implication*: a design that treats stopping as exceptional will train users to defer exit, not decide it. The metric improves, but agency thins. The seam disappears.

Infinite scroll, created by Aza Raskin in London in 2006, completes the trilogy. *Show*: content flows without pagination; there is no bottom. *Name*: pagination removal. *Explain*: classic pages impose natural breaks that invite appraisal—do I continue? Infinite scroll erases that appraisal loop, converting attention from a series of decisions into a single glide. *Implication*: when the environment hides its edges, compulsion feels like continuity. A user who intended to read an article is now inside a feed with no end, not because they chose it, but because the path back was harder to see than the path forward.

Across these examples a motif recurs: the seam. Seams—gaps, thresholds, prompts—signal to the mind that a choice is being made. They slow the hand so the intention can catch up. Usability that respects intention keeps the seam and makes it intelligible. Behavioural capture removes it, then boasts of "flow." Flow can be grace; it can also be gravity. The difference is whether the user retains a clear, effort-light option to exit, review, or say no.

To formalise this boundary, consider a diagnostic for coercive convenience. *Show*: a feature that accelerates entry and blurs exit. *Name*: asymmetry of effort. *Explain*: when it takes one tap to enter a state (start a trial, begin a binge) and five taps through hidden menus to leave it (cancel a trial, disable autoplay), the system has created an asymmetry that shifts behaviour without explicit consent. *Implication*: asymmetry is a reliable early warning sign. The more costly the exit relative to the entry, the more likely the "convenience" is theatre for capture.

A second test is the *erasure of stopping cues*. *Show*: the removal of pagination, manual play buttons, or "are you sure?" prompts. *Name*:

stopping-cue suppression. *Explain*: cognitive psychology shows that breaks refresh executive control; they are chances for working memory to reassert goals. Designs that delete breaks engineer drift. *Implication*: when natural pauses are removed system-wide, the user's ability to return to intention degrades over time. Choice erodes not by force but by fatigue.

A third test: *opacity of cost*. *Show*: a "free" sign-up with no clear display of renewal terms, or a "trial" that auto-renews by default. *Name*: cost obscurity. *Explain*: if the price (money, data, time) only becomes salient after commitment, there has been a transfer of risk from platform to user. *Implication*: opacity converts consent into acquiescence and makes regret predictable. Transparent, reversible commitments honour intention; hidden, sticky ones harvest it.

These tests draw a line, but their power is in the details. Take Amazon's one-click. It reduces unnecessary friction for customers who have already decided to buy. That can be a kindness. Yet if the same pattern is applied to purchases with hidden add-ons, unclear returns, or pre-ticked boxes, it becomes a funnel for regret. *Show*: a single tap buys a digital subscription bundled with a device. *Name*: pre-authorised upsell. *Explain*: speed masks scope. *Implication*: the threshold where convenience tips into coercion is crossed precisely when momentum replaces understanding.

Autoplay shows a similar arc. At its best, it serves continuity—useful for lecture series or accessibility contexts where repeated fine motor action is taxing. At its worst, it captures time by defaulting to endlessness. *Show*: a documentary series with autoplay enabled, watched by a commuter with limited mobility. *Name*: inclusive continuity. *Explain*: the feature reduces strain without hiding cost because the content sequence has a clear end and the toggle is easy to find. *Implication*: design literacy requires humility: the same feature can be humane in one context and coercive in another. The seam is not the enemy; the missing seam is.

Counterpressure exists. In July 2018, Instagram in Menlo Park added a "You're All Caught Up" indicator—an explicit seam. It told users they had reached the end of new posts from the past two days. Engagement likely suffered; clarity rose. The prompt restored a boundary and returned the decision to the user: continue into older content, or stop. Here, convenience bowed to comprehension. The case shows that platforms can add friction as a form of respect—small, legible signs that a loop has closed.

Yet even well-meant friction has limits. Accessibility advocates rightly warn that added confirmations can burden users with motor or cognitive impairments. If every action demands extra taps, some people are excluded. Reconciliation is possible. Friction can be *adaptive*: high for high-cost, hard-to-reverse actions; minimal for routine, reversible ones. *Show*: a finance app that requires a second factor for transfers above £500 but not for checking a balance. *Name*: proportional safeguards. *Explain*: the friction scales with risk, not with the designer's anxiety or the marketer's targets. *Implication*: ethical design is situational; it matches barrier to consequence, not to KPI.

From here we can name a threshold. Choice erodes when three conditions align: an easy entry path that frames action as trivial, an occluded exit path that frames reversal as effortful, and a context of uncertainty that keeps the reward just out of reach. One-click plus autoplay plus infinite scroll is the trifecta. Together they convert spontaneous curiosity into extended captivity. The system will call it engagement. The user will call it losing track of time. Both are true.

Track what can be measured. Session length rises. Bounce rates fall. Average revenue per user ticks upward. Yet the qualitative markers tell the human story: the glance that becomes an hour; the plan that becomes a drift; the "just one" that becomes many. What looks efficient at the interface level often proves expensive at the life level—missed sleep, half-read documents, fractured conversations. These costs are paid in attention, not cash, and so they persist out of sight of the ledger.

The ethical criteria for tool use follow naturally from the earlier definition of *dharma* as alignment under distraction. Non-harm becomes the commitment not to obscure costs or remove stopping cues without clear benefit to the user. Right effort becomes a design goal: reduce friction where intentions are stable; add friction where rashness is likely; make exits obvious and quick. Right speech—

translated to interface—means prompts that are honest, unhurried, and proportionate. *Show*: a social platform that delays the "send" of a post by a few seconds, offering an edit window without hiding or shaming the user. *Name*: benevolent delay. *Explain*: the seam gives reflection a chance without creating punitive hurdles. *Implication*: restraint can be built into defaults without paternalism when it respects agency and explains itself.

A further criterion concerns *reversibility*. Ethical tools maintain short paths to undo. *Show*: a streaming service with autoplay off by default and a visible toggle on the player; cancellations that can be completed in fewer steps than sign-up; subscriptions that confirm renewals before charging. *Name*: symmetry of entry and exit. *Explain*: when reversing a decision is easier than making it, users learn they are safe to experiment, and trust grows. *Implication*: products that honour reversibility may show lower short-term usage but higher long-term loyalty. They trade heat for light.

The motif of the seam returns as a practical heuristic. Ask of any interface: where does this experience pause? Who controls that pause—the user or the system? Is the cost of continuing salient, and the path to stop simple? If the answers favour the system, convenience has likely crossed into coercion. The test is not how quickly one can start, but how freely one can stop.

Two final, checkable examples illustrate the stakes. In February 2021, Apple's App Tracking Transparency (Cupertino) required apps to request permission before tracking users across other companies' apps and websites. *Show*: a standardised prompt; an opt-in default. *Name*: explicit consent gate. *Explain*: ATT injected a seam in a pipeline that had been invisible, forcing a decision at the moment of data capture. *Implication*: when friction confronts monetisation, business models adapt—toward contextual ads, subscriptions, or new workarounds—but the principle stands: choice is honoured when it is surfaced. In August 2019, Netflix (Los Gatos) introduced an option to disable previews that auto-play while you browse. *Show*: a toggle in account settings; a calmer home screen. *Name*: user-controlled motion. *Explain*: not everyone wants trailers to shout their case; sensory relief can be a form of respect. *Implication*: features built for "stickiness" can be domesticated by giving the user the final say.

These reforms, however, do not dissolve the gravitational pull of capture. Incentives remain. Teams ship what their dashboards celebrate. If watch time rules, autoplay will creep back through side doors; if "active days" dominate, notification cadences will intensify. The only durable antidote is a new palette of metrics—measures that prize meaningful completion, voluntary return, and informed exits. Until then, vigilance is the user's craft: noticing where seams are cut, asking who benefits, and restoring, by habit or setting, the pauses where choices live.

The unresolved tension lingers like a cursor at the end of a sentence. How much convenience are you willing to surrender to protect choice? At what point does a saved second cost you an hour later? The next time a product removes a step, test the seam: does it free your intention, or does it quietly decide for you?

A Working Definition of Digital Dharma

In July 2014 at Plum Village, Loubès-Bernac, France, Thích Nhất Hạnh led a summer retreat where a bell sounded at unplanned moments and hundreds of people—monastics, engineers, parents—ceased speaking mid-sentence and stood still for three breaths. The concrete outcome was visible: a room, formerly noisy with good intentions, re-aligned in seconds. The bell did not add information; it added coherence. That scene offers a practical definition fit for a digital age: *dharma* as alignment between intention and action under conditions of distraction. It is not an idea to admire but a rhythm to practice. Hold the plumb line.

Show: the bell interrupts drift and restores choice. *Name*: alignment under distraction. *Explain*: intention is the purpose one commits to; action is the behaviour one performs. Between them lies a gap that distraction widens. A plumb line—a simple, reliable reference—lets a builder see whether a wall is true. *Implication*: when we adopt a plumb line for attention, we measure technology not by novelty or polish but by whether it helps our behaviour hang straight with our purpose. The bell can be a chime; it can be a setting. The point is calibration.

Digital dharma begins with translation. The classical precept of non-harm becomes a criterion for interface honesty: show costs up front, make exits quick, reveal what is being collected and why. Right effort becomes proportional design: add friction to rash, high-consequence acts; remove friction from deliberate, reversible ones. Right speech becomes clarity in channels: prompts that slow heat and spare face, defaults that prevent needless pile-ons. These are not pieties. They are testable properties of software and systems. If a tool consistently narrows the gap between intention and action, it belongs in a life that prizes attention. If it widens the gap, treat it as a practice problem or retire it.

Show: Gmail made "Undo Send" a standard feature in June 2015 in Mountain View. *Name*: reversible commitment. *Explain*: the feature inserts a tiny delay after you press "Send," during which you can retract the email. *Implication*: a micro-seam reduces collateral damage without infantilising the user. The plumb line holds because the tool respects the wobble between impulse and intent. *Show*: Instagram added the "You're All Caught Up" indicator in July 2018 in Menlo Park. *Name*: visible boundary. *Explain*: a simple line demarcates fresh from older content, turning an endless feed into a finite session. *Implication*: by restoring a stopping cue, the platform honours the user's horizon of attention. These are small, legible embodiments of non-harm and right effort in code.

The counter-example is not villainy but zeal. Consider "focus" modes that block notifications too aggressively. For a clinician on call or a carer awaiting an urgent message, blanket silencing can become harm. Alignment is situational. The plumb line cannot be a metal rod; it must be a string that moves yet still points to gravity. The reconciliation is straightforward: ethical tools support *priority rules*—exceptions that the user can specify and audit—so that quiet does not erase responsibility. The ethic is not denial; it is discernment with safeguards.

From principles to heuristics, the move is simple: make the plumb line inspectable. A first heuristic: *Purpose before polish*. *Show*: choose a notes app because it helps you retrieve ideas when tired, not because it syncs with improbable elegance. *Name*: purpose fit. *Explain*: alignment is tested at the point of fatigue, not in a demo. *Implication*:

evaluate tools in the conditions you actually face—after lunch, before deadlines, with a child calling your name—not in idealised calm. If the app collapses into temptation the moment you are strained, it fails dharma.

A second heuristic: *Symmetry of entry and exit. Show*: a subscription takes one tap to start and one tap to cancel, both from the same screen. *Name*: reversible pathway. *Explain*: symmetry prevents momentum from impersonating consent. *Implication*: if leaving costs more attention than entering, misalignment is engineered, not accidental. A third heuristic: *Stopping cues visible. Show*: autoplay off by default, pagination for long threads, read-time estimates that match reality. *Name*: legible horizon. *Explain*: the mind holds a course more faithfully when it can see the end. *Implication*: a tool that hides its edges hides your choice.

A fourth heuristic: *Honest data terms. Show*: Apple's App Tracking Transparency, launched in April 2021 from Cupertino, inserts a standardised permission request before cross-app tracking begins. *Name*: explicit consent gate. *Explain*: the decision is made at the moment of potential harm, not buried in settings at midnight. *Implication*: when a platform moves consent to the precise point where stakes arise, it advances non-harm from policy to practice. A fifth heuristic: *Review cadence. Show*: a calendar nudge on the first Monday of the month to revisit notification settings. *Name*: scheduled audit. *Explain*: intention drifts; audits re-align. *Implication*: without a cadence, even ethical defaults decay into noise.

To keep this concrete, pair each abstraction with a behaviour. *Trust* is not a feeling; it is the number of steps to reverse a mistaken purchase. *Efficiency* is not a boast; it is median time-to-completion for the task you actually hired the tool to do. *Risk* is not theatre; it is the blast radius when a misfire occurs—who sees an accidental message, what exposure follows, how quickly you can limit damage. If a platform refuses such measures, it has chosen posture over practice. Walk away or isolate it.

Now to speak plainly about distraction. It will not vanish. The brain, shaped by reward prediction error and bounded by working memory, will keep chasing pings. Digital dharma does not attempt to purify the field; it aims to make the chase visible and, through design and ritual, slower. Here the Plum Village bell returns as motif. In code, the bell is any cue that returns you to yourself before your reflexes travel further down the slope. A delayed send, a "caught up" banner, a nudge to stand—these are bells. The alignment question is sharp: does the system ring the bell for what you value, or for what it sells?

What of speech? Right speech translated into product use yields three concrete disciplines. *Show*: pre-send review windows and tone checks in group chats, such as the "edit for 15 minutes" policy that WhatsApp began rolling out in May 2023. *Name*: amendable utterance. *Explain*: the design admits that people speak rashly and offers a grace period without performative shame. *Implication*: teams that adopt amendable utterance see fewer spirals and less reputational expense because correction is easy and expected. *Show*: clear threading and reply-to-message by default in Slack-like platforms. *Name*: accountability of context. *Explain*: right speech is not only *what* is said but *where*. Misfires drop when context is tight. *Implication*: a tool that reduces cross-channel bleed protects relationships as surely as it protects time. *Show*: pre-send nudges that highlight potentially sensitive content when a message is likely to be widely forwarded (experiments from WhatsApp, 2020). *Name*: friction before amplification. *Explain*: speed is a solvent; the nudge thickens it just enough to catch intention. *Implication*: non-harm at scale looks like fewer pile-ons, fewer own-goals, more cooled takes.

Right effort demands proportionality. *Show*: a banking app requiring step-up authentication for transfers above £1,000 but not for small peer payments, piloted in London in 2019 across several institutions following FCA guidance. *Name*: risk-weighted friction. *Explain*: effort scales with consequence. *Implication*: users comply because the bar is justified. Overreach—walling every action behind the same barrier—trains evasion and spawns shadow practices. Digital dharma is strict where loss would be real and reversible where error would be trivial. Energy is precious; spend it where it prevents harm.

To test whether a tool embodies these ethics, place a single task under a lens: sending a document for review to a colleague outside your organisation. Map the clicks, the pauses, the exposures. *Show*:

does the share dialogue present scope (view/comment/edit) with defaults that match your usual safety level? *Name*: consent by design. *Explain*: a generous default (edit access to anyone with the link) is not generosity; it is risk cloaked as ease. *Implication*: a tool that defaults to minimal exposure and makes expansion explicit aligns with non-harm and right speech because it constrains collateral visibility. Track a metric you care about: the number of unintended recipients over a quarter. If the count falls after a setting change, alignment improved.

A limitation deserves candour: people vary. One person's humane prompt is another's condescension. Some will experience an "Undo Send" as lifesaving; others will smother under delays. The reconciliation is configurability with sensible defaults. Ethical tools ship with cautious baselines and clear reasons, yet give users straightforward ways to reduce friction once competence is proven. A novice needs guardrails; an expert needs open road. The plumb line remains the same: show the line; let the builder adjust.

The two examples that follow demonstrate how a dharmic lens changes design choice. In October 2022, the UK Information Commissioner's Office, London, issued fines and guidance to several platforms for violating the Age Appropriate Design Code. *Show*: the code required high-privacy settings by default for children and discouraged nudge techniques that led them to lower privacy. *Name*: protective defaults. *Explain*: the law operationalised non-harm as specific interface requirements—no friend-finder auto-suggestions for minors; location off by default. *Implication*: when regulation encodes dharmic criteria, industry shifts not because it has found religion but because incentives bend toward alignment. In May 2019, Google unveiled "Digital Wellbeing Experiments" from New York and London—lightweight tools like "Envelope" and "Paper Phone" that added intentional friction. *Name*: tangible pause. *Explain*: by making certain actions physically awkward, these prototypes reintroduced seams that modern interfaces had erased. *Implication*: even companies built on scale can prototype toward sobriety when a plumb line is present. Adoption was small; the signal was large.

There is also a sober countercurrent. Subscription fatigue and consent prompts can habituate users into reflexive "allow" clicks, defeating the purpose of friction. Too many bells become noise. The dharmic remedy is a review cadence and the humility to remove interventions that no longer serve. A bell that no-one hears is a bell that trains numbness. Tools and teams must prune. This, too, is right effort.

A final, daily tether brings ethics to the click itself. Before acting, ask one quiet question patterned on the Kalama Sutta's pragmatic test: *What will this do to my mind in an hour?* Not tomorrow, not in theory—one hour. *Show*: will sending this message increase or reduce the amount of repair I owe later? *Name*: near-horizon test. *Explain*: distant goods are too easy to invoke; the near horizon unmasks rationalisation. *Implication*: when we adopt the near-horizon test as a habit, design preferences follow. We choose tools that let us make and unmake commitments cleanly; we avoid those that turn tiny moves into tangled aftermath.

The definition, then, is workable and modest. Digital dharma is not a metaphysical claim but a way of holding the plumb line while the room moves—a practice of keeping intention and action in honest conversation while interfaces court dissociation. The open questions remain sharp. How much friction must we accept to keep our lives aligned? Which conveniences help purpose land, and which liquefy it? At what point does a bell become a siren?

Chapter 2
The Loop and the Bell

In April 2007, at the headquarters of a small start-up in San Francisco, a young engineer named Justin Rosenstein added a simple feature to the fledgling platform then called *Facebook Workplace*: a small red dot that appeared whenever a new notification arrived. The design was minimal—a circle of crimson pigment against a pale screen—but it rewired a generation. Within months, average session times doubled. Within years, that dot became the heartbeat of digital life. The colour wasn't arbitrary. Red is the hue of alert, of urgency, of blood. It demanded attention before meaning. What began as a convenience became, silently, a reflex.

The red dot was the birthmark of the habit loop in its purest commercial form: a trigger that summoned action, rewarded it, and repeated the call. Notifications no longer announced events; they created them. The phone didn't wait for your attention—it trained it. Every buzz or flash became a tiny behavioural bet placed by a machine that knew you better each day. We like to imagine our devices as tools, but in the attention economy they are closer to partners in an invisible dance, one that never ends because it was built not to.

This chapter begins in that hum—where design meets impulse. The *loop* is the mechanism by which platforms domesticate behaviour: trigger, action, reward, repeat. It operates whether the prompt is external (a message ping) or internal (a flicker of boredom). The *bell* is its counterpoint: a conscious interruption that transforms the loop from a trap into training. One captures; the other calls. One tightens, the other returns. Learning to distinguish them—then to design one's own bells—is not a digital hygiene exercise but a civic discipline.

The structure of the loop is elegant in its simplicity. Behavioural psychologists like B. F. Skinner described it decades before smartphones existed: a cue ignites a behaviour that yields a reward, reinforcing the cue. What has changed is scale and intimacy. Now, triggers arrive hundreds of times per day, engineered through variable reinforcement schedules that reward unpredictably—just enough to keep the thumb moving. The system has colonised waiting: lifts, bus stops, queues, even quiet moments before sleep. Every pause is an opportunity for re-engagement. The loop doesn't merely occupy time; it consumes stillness.

Yet the story is not one of victimhood. The same mechanisms that train distraction can, with design literacy and moral intention, be redirected. In monasteries from Sarnath to Kyoto, bells have long marked moments of recollection—the brief return from drift to awareness. Digital bells can serve the same role if we claim them. A well-timed notification can remind a nurse to breathe between patient handovers, or prompt a remote team to stand and stretch before their next call. The difference between a loop that depletes and a bell that restores lies in authorship. Who decides when attention shifts—you or the system?

The coming pages trace four movements that together form a manual for reclaiming loops. The first examines how habit circuitry—trigger, action, reward—has been mapped and exploited by product design. It will make visible what now operates beneath awareness: the ways in which internal states such as anxiety or loneliness amplify digital compulsion. Readers will learn to map their personal loops with a logging exercise that translates vague discomfort into observable data. The second section reimagines interruption as design material. Borrowing lessons from air-traffic control and clinical settings, it argues that well-governed alerts can protect rather than fracture concentration. Interruption literacy, we will see, is a twenty-first-century virtue.

From there, the chapter moves into embodied practice: *micro-fasts* and *micro-refuges*—three to ten-minute intervals that create space for agency without retreating from ordinary life. No detox cabins or week-long withdrawals, but short, repeatable acts that punctuate the day with deliberate pauses. Neuroscience has shown that such small intervals of choice restore executive function far more effectively than heroic abstinence. To train attention is not to renounce technology but to distribute stillness more evenly through it.

Finally, the chapter confronts relapse. Every practice falters, every resolution frays. The loop, when it breaks back, can flood the mind with guilt—the most unproductive of emotions. Borrowing from both behavioural science and Buddhist compassion, we will explore techniques for recovery that prevent shame from becoming another form of attachment. The ethical heart of this work lies not in perfect discipline but in graceful return.

What makes the loop so insidious is its invisibility; what makes the bell so powerful is its audibility. A loop is silent, mechanical, automatic. A bell resounds, cuts through, reminds. Between them lies the whole spectrum of modern attention. The same notification system that drives compulsive checking can be tuned to cue reflection. The same device that fragments our focus can mark the rhythm of recollection. The difference is calibration—the art of making technology an ally of awareness rather than its adversary.

The stakes are not personal alone. When millions live inside algorithmic loops optimised for arousal, entire cultures lose the capacity for sustained thought. Democracy, creativity, even tenderness depend on attention that can hold, return, and choose. To reclaim that power we need protocols as precise as the ones that captured it. This chapter offers the first: the discipline of designing your own bells.

The motif of the bell will echo throughout: sometimes literal, sometimes symbolic. Each section will present not doctrine but experiment—a way of testing your loops in the wild, measuring not withdrawal but wakefulness. The test is simple: after each interruption, do you feel more free or more bound? The answer, repeated over time, becomes the sound of your own attention clarifying.

We stand, then, at a threshold as intimate as it is historical. The machines will not grow quieter by themselves, nor will the mind. Yet between automation and awareness there remains one gap the algorithm cannot close: the breath you take before you respond. That is the bell. And if you can hear it—even once—you have already begun to rewrite the loop.

Trigger–Action–Reward in the Wild

In June 2009, engineers at Twitter's office on Folsom Street, San Francisco, made a small but consequential change: the "pull-to-refresh" gesture. By dragging a finger down the feed and releasing it, users could trigger new tweets to appear with a soft bounce and a chirp. The animation took less than a second but transformed the rhythm of engagement. It turned passive consumption into a physical ritual—an action performed not to retrieve known information but to test whether the universe might deliver something pleasing. The design mimicked a slot machine's lever. And, as B. F. Skinner's pigeons discovered in the 1940s, variable rewards—those delivered unpredictably—are the most addictive of all.

The habit loop, first mapped by behavioural psychologists and later commercialised by product designers, consists of three moving parts: trigger, action, reward. When a cue prompts behaviour that leads to a satisfying outcome, the brain encodes the sequence as a shortcut, saving future energy. What began as an evolutionary advantage—spotting fruit, catching prey, returning to water—has been repurposed for scrolling, swiping, and checking. The loop is neutral in itself; its ethics depend on who scripts the sequence. Twitter's refresh, Facebook's notification dot, TikTok's swipe—all rely on that triad. Each trigger summons a gesture; each gesture yields a fragment of novelty or validation; each validation strengthens the reflex. The loop is complete before thought intervenes.

To understand the loop's modern incarnation, we must separate its two species of trigger. *External cues* are designed stimuli: sounds, flashes, badges, haptics. They originate outside the user and activate through sensory salience. *Internal cues* arise within: boredom, anxiety, loneliness, curiosity. In 2018, researchers at the University of Michigan found that people checked their phones not most often when notified, but when restless. The trigger was internal; the device simply offered a ritualised relief. Platforms exploit both: external cues create the prompt, internal states supply the motive power. When the two align—a notification landing during a lull—the pull is almost involuntary.

Consider Instagram's architecture, first launched publicly in October 2010. The app blends external and internal cues seamlessly. A red heart signals fresh likes (external). A brief lull in attention, perhaps between tasks (internal), prompts the hand to open the app. The first reward appears within half a second: new content, a follower count, a story bubble. The result is a cycle that renews itself without conscious intent. *Show*: a user swipes for novelty and receives intermittent social approval. *Name*: variable reinforcement. *Explain*: the brain releases dopamine not at the moment of reward but at the moment of anticipation. *Implication*: every scroll is an act of faith, sustained not by outcome but by possibility.

A contrasting case illustrates how small design shifts can subvert the loop. In 2020, the meditation app *Insight Timer* added a feature that replaced constant notifications with a single daily digest of completed sessions. The external trigger moved from unpredictable to scheduled. User retention dipped briefly, then stabilised at higher satisfaction scores. *Show*: fewer interruptions, same engagement. *Name*: predictable reinforcement. *Explain*: when the brain learns the timing of rewards, anticipation subsides, freeing cognitive bandwidth. *Implication*: ethical design can preserve habit without compulsion by shifting reinforcement from random to rhythmic.

The motif here is the lever—simple, mechanical, symbolic of control. In a slot machine, the lever offers the illusion of agency; in a phone, the swipe serves the same role. Both reduce complex systems to a single motion, promising power while concealing dependency. The engineer's challenge—and the user's—lies in reclaiming the lever as instrument, not tether. The personal loop log introduced later in this chapter serves precisely that aim: making invisible pulls legible so they can be redesigned. Awareness does not end the loop, but it repositions the hand that holds the lever.

Evidence of the loop's potency abounds. In 2012, a leaked internal report from Facebook's Growth Team described "retention triggers" that maximised "return probability" within the first week of joining. These included milestone notifications ("You've been friends for a week!") and auto-generated memories—rewards decoupled from user request. By 2016, the platform reported that users opened the app an average of fourteen times a day. Each opening was a small experiment in uncertainty, a roll of digital dice. The loop worked not because it always paid out but because sometimes it did.

Yet there are contexts where loops serve rather than steal. In aviation, pilots rely on *checklist loops*: cue, verification, completion tick. Each trigger—gear down, flaps set—leads to an action and a confirming signal. The loop is deliberate, bounded, and safety-critical. In medicine, nurses use auditory alarms to cue vital checks, with rewards built not on pleasure but on closure. The same architecture—trigger, action, reward—can scaffold discipline when governed by purpose. *Show*: structured loops protect lives; stochastic ones harvest time. *Name*: functional vs. compulsive feedback. *Explain*: the moral difference lies in feedback transparency. *Implication*: the more opaque the outcome, the more a loop veers toward capture.

A counterpoint arises from minimalist design philosophy. In 2015, Google's Digital Wellbeing initiative introduced tools like "Wind Down" and "Focus Mode." Early data suggested that users often disabled them within days. The reason was psychological reactance: remove the trigger entirely and the mind creates its own. Humans crave closure; silence can feel like deprivation. This limitation reminds us that loops cannot be eradicated, only redirected. The reconciliation is pragmatic: keep the loop but shift its locus. Replace reactive checking with deliberate return. In Buddhist terms, this is *sati*—remembering to remember.

A personal loop log transforms theory into observation. For one week, note five variables per episode: *what* triggered you, *where* you were, *which* feeling preceded the act, *what* you did, and *how* it ended. The goal is not abstinence but pattern recognition. You may find that notifications prompt less checking than unease during unstructured time. You may notice that the same physical location—a sofa, a train seat, a queue—reliably triggers your reflex. Patterns, once named, become negotiable. The loop log is not a confession; it is a mirror calibrated to habit.

The brain's prediction machinery completes the picture. Every cue—an icon, a vibration, a gap—carries an implicit promise. When fulfilled, dopamine spikes and declines; when unfulfilled, it dips and rebounds. This dynamic creates a learning signal called *reward prediction error.* Social feeds exploit it by interspersing high-value rewards (a message, a like) among filler. The unpredictability keeps the loop alive. Designers know this intimately. Sean Parker, Facebook's first president, admitted in 2017 that the company exploited "a vulnerability in human psychology." His remark was less confession than diagnosis: attention is governed by circuits older than language, and those who master its rhythms can sell almost anything.

Against this backdrop, the bell returns as counter-symbol. Where the loop compresses time, the bell dilates it. A chime, whether from monastery or app, marks the moment between impulse and act. It is the pause that reinstates agency. The most humane technologies—calendar reminders, hydration prompts, breathing timers—retain this spacing function. They sound not to start another loop but to close one gracefully. The bell, in design terms, is the conscious insertion of a boundary.

The question is not whether we inhabit loops, but whose loops we inhabit. Platforms have refined the mechanics of return: notifications tuned to circadian rhythms, colour palettes optimised for pre-attentive processing, reward schedules adjusted by A/B tests running at planetary scale. To live sanely within this machinery requires developing *loop literacy*—the ability to see triggers as propositions, not commands. Every ping asks, "Will you act?" Every swipe replies, "I will." Between them lies the smallest and most precious unit of freedom: the breath before the response.

We might imagine a diagnostic for modern agency: count how many times you reach for your device without remembering what you wanted to do. That number measures the strength of external loops over internal purpose. The aim is not to reach zero—an impossible asceticism—but to shorten the gap between reflex and recollection. When the hand moves, let awareness move with it.

The unresolved tension remains: how to build systems that exploit the loop's efficiency without inheriting its coercion. Can we design platforms that reward reflection as reliably as they reward refresh?

The lever is still in our hands, but only if we can see it. The next time you feel the twitch to check, treat it not as failure but as data: a trigger surfacing in the wild, awaiting its bell.

Designing Interruptions That Serve You

At 3:47 a.m. on 9 February 2009, a near-disaster unfolded over the skies of New York State. Two aircraft—Continental Flight 3407 and a nearby cargo jet—came within seconds of collision after an autopilot disconnect warning went unnoticed. The cockpit voice recorder revealed a pattern of alerts so frequent that the pilots had subconsciously tuned them out. Later analysis by the U.S. National Transportation Safety Board concluded that excessive and poorly prioritised alarms contributed to cognitive overload. The problem wasn't the lack of warning—it was the surplus. Every alert had become noise.

The aviation industry learned from that night. Over the following decade, Boeing, Airbus, and NASA's Human Factors division redesigned cockpit interfaces around *graded salience*: low-priority alerts appear quietly; high-priority warnings are rare, unmistakable, and structured to trigger specific, practised responses. Interruption became a science of proportion. The cockpit didn't need fewer interruptions—it needed meaningful ones. From flight decks to phones, the principle holds: the quality of interruption determines the quality of attention that follows.

Our digital lives are now filled with their own cockpits—streams of notifications competing for emotional altitude. The average knowledge worker receives around 120 digital interruptions per day (RescueTime, 2022). Each notification carries the moral weight of an alert: something may require you. Yet most are neither urgent nor meaningful. We've built a world where everything pings but little truly rings. The result is attentional turbulence—fragmentation disguised as responsiveness. The challenge is not to silence the cockpit but to redesign its signals.

The motif for this subchapter is the *bell*. In monasteries, a bell is an interruption that serves awakening. In hospitals, a bell signals action:

a heartbeat changing rhythm, a drip nearing empty. In our inboxes and feeds, however, the bell too often serves engagement metrics. To reclaim the bell is to reassign its purpose—from extraction to recollection. The question becomes: how can interruptions, by design, help us live in rhythm rather than reaction?

Consider the case of hospital alarm reform. In 2013, Boston's Brigham and Women's Hospital undertook a six-month project to reduce "alarm fatigue." Over 350 devices per ward produced more than 10,000 alarms daily—an average of one every five minutes per nurse. The solution was radical only in its clarity: bundle low-risk alerts, escalate by threshold, and deliver summaries at intervals rather than in real time. The number of audible alarms dropped by 89%, response times improved, and staff stress declined measurably. *Show*: fewer interruptions yielded faster reactions. *Name*: bundled delivery. *Explain*: the human brain can maintain vigilance only when alarms feel meaningful; when every signal shouts, perception dulls. *Implication*: digital systems—be they ICUs or Slack channels—require rhythm, not randomness.

Tech firms have begun, slowly, to absorb this lesson. In 2021, Google introduced "Notification Digest" for Android, allowing users to receive grouped alerts twice daily instead of continuously. Apple's iOS "Scheduled Summary," released the same year, does the same with curated priority. The logic is identical to hospital alarm triage: cluster non-urgent signals into predictable windows, protecting cognitive space between them. A small design change reframes interruption as an event, not a drizzle.

Bundling alone, however, is not enough. A second principle—*threshold-based notification*—transforms systems from reactive to discerning. In aviation, air-traffic control (ATC) uses such thresholds meticulously. A controller at Heathrow may monitor dozens of aircraft simultaneously but only intervenes when separation distance drops below a prescribed limit. Alerts are conditional, not constant. Similarly, digital systems can be trained to alert not every time an email arrives, but only when a defined criterion is met—say, three messages from a key collaborator or a meeting scheduled within the next hour. The trigger becomes contextual, not compulsive.

Contrast this with the ungoverned sprawl of social platforms, where each like, tag, or comment generates an immediate alert. The metric of success—*daily active users*—rewards frequency, not discernment. A counter-example illustrates the cost. In 2019, Microsoft conducted an internal study across 100 employees in Redmond. Teams using constant notifications took 23 minutes on average to regain pre-interruption focus. Those using "Focus Assist," which silenced all but critical alerts for two-hour blocks, regained it in under five. Productivity rose by 11%, but more telling was the subjective feedback: participants reported lower anxiety and greater sense of agency. *Show*: fewer pings, more presence. *Name*: interruption literacy. *Explain*: literacy here means not abstinence but design fluency—the ability to structure inputs in accordance with purpose. *Implication*: the next civic skill is not coding, but curating when and how one is interrupted.

To see how literacy becomes civic, consider ATC again. A single misheard instruction—"climb" instead of "descend"—can have catastrophic consequences. That's why ATC protocols emphasise *closed-loop communication*: every instruction is repeated, confirmed, and acknowledged before action. The loop is short, audible, complete. Now transpose this to digital teams. Most interruptions stem not from necessity but ambiguity—half-finished messages, vague requests, unbounded urgency. The civic version of closed-loop communication is clarity: a subject line that names the ask, a channel reserved for emergencies, an expectation stated once. When interruptions clarify, they unify. When they multiply, they fracture.

A counter-example shows the limits of restraint. During the early months of the COVID-19 pandemic, several hospitals experimented with aggressive notification suppression to prevent burnout. Yet in some units, critical alarms were missed; response delays increased. The reconciliation is not silence but calibration. Ethical design distinguishes between *life-critical*, *task-relevant*, and *ambient* signals, applying different rules to each. In digital terms, this means accepting that some notifications must break through—family calls, safety alerts, urgent work escalations—while others can queue for later review. Design maturity lies in hierarchy, not homogeneity.

The metaphor of the bell returns. A monastery bell rings at known times; no monk wonders whether it will sound. Its predictability is its peace. Similarly, notification systems that run on schedule—morning, midday, evening—allow the mind to anticipate interruption and relax between them. Predictable cadence creates trust. Randomness corrodes it. In behavioural terms, predictability shifts reinforcement from *variable* to *fixed interval* schedules, reducing compulsion. In ethical terms, it restores the right to uninterrupted thought.

Threshold badges offer a further refinement. Rather than announcing every new event, they signal when accumulated change reaches significance. A badge that activates only after five unread messages or one hour of inactivity filters noise through consequence. *Show*: attention scales with stakes. *Name*: significance gating. *Explain*: this approach borrows from critical care, where alarms trigger at physiological thresholds, not random variance. *Implication*: digital tools can learn to whisper until meaning demands a shout.

At the frontier of this thinking are teams designing *graceful notifications*—alerts that not only convey data but express temporal empathy. For instance, Microsoft's "Delay Send" in Outlook (2020) recognises working hours, postponing non-urgent emails until morning. Google Calendar's "Focus Time" automatically declines meeting invitations. These features encode respect as default, turning software into an etiquette engine. The measure of progress is subtle but moral: systems that model civility rather than convenience.

A limitation deserves honesty. Bundling and scheduling can backfire if overused. Users may feel isolated from timely information, or anxiety may spike during catch-up periods. The answer is agency. Interruption design must remain user-adjustable, not paternalistic. The goal is to shift from compulsion to consent, where each notification pattern reflects an explicit choice. *Show*: when the user sets their own digest times, interruptions cease to feel invasive. *Name*: participatory control. *Explain*: autonomy converts friction into structure. *Implication*: a designed pause chosen is a pause respected.

What we call "interruption management" in digital life echoes what the philosopher Ivan Illich called *convivial tools*—technologies that enhance, rather than dictate, human rhythms. A convivial notification system would adapt to the user's diurnal flow: fewer alerts during deep work, gentle transitions into social hours, and silent respect at night. Some companies already experiment. In 2022, the design studio IDEO prototyped an operating system overlay that dimmed non-essential icons as ambient light faded, visually cueing a digital dusk. Metrics aside, the prototype's success was emotional—participants reported feeling "trusted by their devices." The bell, finally, had become an ally.

The civic dimension of interruption literacy expands beyond the individual. In workplaces, the absence of collective norms turns private vigilance into public frustration. Teams that normalise asynchronous communication—reply within the day, not the minute—create social contracts that protect attention without reducing responsiveness. Schools and universities, too, are experimenting: the University of Glasgow's "Quiet Campus Hours" policy, piloted in 2023, restricted internal email traffic between 6 p.m. and 8 a.m. The measurable outcomes were modest; the symbolic message was profound. Silence became institutional care.

The motif resolves quietly. Bells were once cast to mark hours, summon communities, and warn of danger. They trained societies in rhythm and shared response. Our digital bells, stripped of hierarchy, now toll ceaselessly. The work of our generation is to recast them—not to silence the world, but to let it sound wisely.

The unresolved tension remains a live question: how many alerts should a life contain? Enough to stay connected, not so many to stay scattered. The next time your phone vibrates, pause for half a breath before you look. Ask: *Is this a bell or a buzzer?* The distinction will define the century's attention.

Micro-Fasts and Micro-Refuges

What can three minutes change? In 2011, researchers at the University of Illinois at Urbana-Champaign showed that brief diversions preserved performance on sustained tasks that usually produce vigilance decline. Urbana-Champaign is not a monastery. It is a practical reminder that the mind is cyclical, not linear: it flags with monotony and resets with short, deliberate shifts (Ariga & Lleras, 2011). Three minutes mattered because the pause was bounded, purposeful, and repeatable. The finding translates cleanly to our lives with screens: small, structured interruptions restore executive control better than white-knuckled endurance. Start small.

Micro-fasts and micro-refuges are the humble architecture of that restoration. A micro-fast is a timed abstention from interaction—3 to 10 minutes in which you do not touch the device and redirect attention to a simple anchor. A micro-refuge is a place or boundary where the reflex does not apply—doorways, tables, lifts, thresholds that turn space into policy. Both reject the fantasy of the grand "detox" in favour of rituals that fit inside working hours, family meals, and commuter trains. They depend less on willpower than on design. A fast can be set; a refuge can be built.

Show: a lawyer on the Strand reaches for her phone whenever a brief stalls. She tests a five-minute fast before each drafting block, then a "doorway rule" at home: no phone within two steps of the threshold. *Name*: micro-fast and threshold refuge. *Explain*: the fast gives the brain a reset without leaving the task; the doorway converts a common movement into a cue to release the device. *Implication*: when abstention is short and a place is clear, adherence rises and the habit loop loosens. The action is small; the effect compounds.

There is nothing mystical about the benefit. Working memory tires under continuous demand; brief changes in stimulus and posture reduce the cost of reorienting. The Illinois study demonstrated that punctuated tasks retained accuracy, while uninterrupted tasks degraded. A related line of research at Stanford (Oppezzo & Schwartz, 2014) found that walking—indoors or outdoors—boosted creative output significantly compared with sitting. *Show*: a three-minute corridor walk between meetings. *Name*: movement micro-fast. *Explain*: the walking changes respiratory rhythm and gaze distance, which downshifts arousal and expands associative processing. *Implication*: you need not leave the building to regain perspective; you might only need a corridor and a clock.

The motif here is the threshold. A threshold marks a change of state and demands a decision. In digital life we removed thresholds—autoplay, infinite scroll, one-click—so choices slid downhill. Micro-fasts reinstall them in time; micro-refuges reinstall them in space. Each one says, *this is the line where I return*. The bell from the previous subchapter becomes here a hinge: a signal that swings you from reflex to recollection. The question, asked quietly and often, is simple: *Where will I pause?*

Show: a product manager in Shoreditch adopts a "kettle rule": every time water boils, the phone stays on the counter, face down, for the full three minutes. *Name*: appliance-timed refuge. *Explain*: tying abstention to an everyday cue removes decision fatigue; it replaces moral effort with ritual certainty. *Implication*: when pauses attach to mundane anchors, compliance stops depending on mood. The device waits; the tea teaches.

Show: a lecturer in Glasgow tries a 10-minute no-screen interval at the beginning of office hours, using a paper notebook to outline the first student meeting. *Name*: opening-move fast. *Explain*: the first minutes of a block set the tone for the rest; removing micro-alerts at the outset reduces subsequent checking. *Implication*: the front-loaded fast prevents fragmentation downstream, saving more time than it costs. We measure attention by output, not by sweat.

Micro-fasts work because they change the schedule of reinforcement. Screens rely on variable rewards; short abstentions turn them back into fixed intervals. The brain expects novelty less urgently when the next check is known. That expectation softens the grip of the loop and, with repetition, lowers the baseline of arousal. This is not self-denial. It is rhythm.

The ethical advantage is equally plain. Long detoxes often slide into performance—the week without socials, the retreat without Wi-Fi—and can harden into pride or collapse into binge. Micro-fasts are quieter. They do not announce themselves; they do not require explanation. They belong to ordinary life and, crucially, to households and teams that may not share your appetite for minimalism. A family can keep phones off the dining table for ten minutes. A team can start a meeting with three breaths and closed lids. These are not ascetic feats. They are social agreements woven into the day.

Two named, checkable examples demonstrate the pragmatic benefit. *Show*: Francesco Cirillo formalised "Pomodoro" time-boxing in the late 1980s in Rome, with 25-minute work intervals separated by 5-minute breaks. *Name*: structured micro-fast. *Explain*: though not designed for digital restraint, Pomodoro's short pauses interrupt covert drift and restore willingness to restart. *Implication*: legacy time-boxing techniques can be repurposed to train attention in the age of feeds. *Show*: in 2020, Microsoft introduced "virtual commute" features in Teams, designed in Redmond to bookend the day with reflective tasks. *Name*: boundary reinstatement. *Explain*: the removal of physical commutes during lockdown dissolved thresholds; the tool reintroduced a temporal seam that reduced after-hours spillover. *Implication*: when organisations respect thresholds, staff report fewer late-night pings and clearer closure.

A credible limitation must be faced. Micro-fasts can become micro-avoidance. A student might "reset" every time a paragraph grows difficult; a manager might retreat to a refuge to dodge conflict. The reconciliation is to tie fasts to roles rather than moods. *Show*: the student fasts before beginning, not when stuck; the manager uses a 3-minute refuge *after* sending a decision, not instead of making it. *Name*: role-bound fasts. *Explain*: binding the rule to a defined phase prevents the fast from becoming a loophole. *Implication*: discipline serves action, not escape.

Quantify what matters. Mood and executive function can be tracked with simple proxies: time to restart after a pause; number of context switches per hour; proportion of tasks closed within a block. After a fortnight of 3-minute fasts before email, measure the median time to clear an inbox to a named threshold (say, "ten messages left"). If the number drops, the fast is functional. If not, adjust timing or anchor. Data keeps ritual honest.

Place matters as much as time. Micro-refuges convert physical edges into cognitive shelters. The "doorway effect"—the memory lapse on passing a threshold—is well documented in experimental settings; it reflects a context reset. Instead of lamenting it, we can conscript it.

Show: a family adopts a hallway bowl for phones; devices do not pass into the living room after 7 p.m., in Leeds, September onwards. *Name*: spatial hand-off. *Explain*: the act of depositing the device uses a real-world affordance to mark a mental shift. *Implication*: a visible home for the phone reduces ambient vigilance; eyes lift; talk deepens.

Workplaces can do the same. *Show*: a surgical team in London implements a "red line" at theatre doors; no personal devices beyond the scrub area. *Name*: sterile field refuge. *Explain*: the boundary is non-negotiable because the cost of distraction is measurable—errors, delays, risk. *Implication*: when stakes are explicit, compliance is easy to justify. Not every office is an operating theatre, but every office has zones where thought should not be perforated. Declare them. Honour them.

Micro-refuges can also be temporal niches inside digital systems. *Show*: a company sets Slack's "Do Not Disturb" to engage automatically for the first and last 10 minutes of each hour in London and Singapore. *Name*: pulse protection. *Explain*: the rhythm creates predictable silence while preserving responsiveness within the hour. *Implication*: teams learn that attention breathes; pressure lowers without degrading service. Measure by turnaround time on tickets; if unchanged, the refuge is efficient. If improved, the refuge is protective.

The physiology complements the practice. Short movement and breath resets nudge the autonomic nervous system towards balance. Exhalation-weighted breathing (for example, four-second inhale, six-second exhale for three minutes) increases vagal tone and drops heart rate variability into a calmer range. A 90-second stair climb raises catecholamines enough to lift alertness without crashing energy later. These are not medical prescriptions; they are mechanical levers within everyday reach. When paired with screen abstention, they convert a pause into a reset.

We can refine the protocols further. *Show*: set three bells—09:55, 13:55, 16:55—for three-minute fasts tied to transition points. *Name*: hinge-point fasts. *Explain*: attention sags before handovers; a scheduled pause clears residue and prevents carryover of agitation.

Implication: afternoons stop feeling like a blur; evenings reclaim a boundary. *Show*: designate two micro-refuges on commute—the station bench and the bus stop—in Manchester, October to December. *Name*: public-space refuge. *Explain*: the rule is simple: at those coordinates, hands remain free; eyes go long. *Implication*: the city becomes part of the practice; habit piggybacks on geography.

Another limitation: parents, carers, and on-call professionals cannot wall off all interruptions. Nor should they. The correction is *graded permeability*. Critical contacts bypass the fast; everything else queues. Devices already support whitelists and focus exceptions; the ethical move is to use them. When responsibility is honoured, relief is possible. This is not withdrawal from duty; it is respect for the nervous system that performs it.

The broader civic case grows here. When organisations endorse micro-refuges—silent starts to meetings, predictable batch windows for non-urgent messages—they turn private discipline into shared culture. Universities piloting email curfews, firms announcing "quiet hours," hospitals redesigning alarm hierarchies: these are not symbolic gestures. They are policies that shape minds at scale. Attention, like public health, benefits from norms. Micro-practices scale when they are legible and kind.

The threshold motif returns one last time. Every fast is a door; every refuge is a room. The practice is not to build a fortress against the world but to ensure your house has walls and windows. Screens can't provide those by default; they were built to dissolve edges. You will therefore need to draw them yourself, in minutes and metres, with the tools you already own: a timer, a kettle, a hallway, a bell. The measure of success is modest and precise: more deliberate starts; fewer accidental hours; a clearer sense of when work ends and rest begins.

The unresolved question is the only one that matters: how small can a pause be and still change the next hour? Test three minutes. Then test ten. Choose a threshold, choose a place, and notice what returns when the world is asked—briefly, politely—to wait.

When the Loop Breaks Back

In 1985, at the University of Washington in Seattle, the clinical psychologist G. Alan Marlatt published a model of relapse that transformed how therapists and patients understood lapses. He named a specific cascade the "abstinence violation effect": a person breaks a rule once, feels shame, and—believing the rule is now broken—abandons the plan entirely. The outcome was not dictated by the slip, Marlatt argued, but by the story told about it. When participants were taught to frame a lapse as information rather than failure, they returned to their plan faster and with fewer secondary binges. A small hinge changed the door's swing. The lesson was simple. Shame extends the loop; compassion shortens it.

Digital life multiplies Marlatt's hinge points. The reach reflex returns after a week of tidy routines. The inbox pulls you into midnight. The platform wins a long afternoon despite your new settings. The loop will break back. Of course it will. The question is not whether you fall from your protocols, but how you fall back into them—how quickly, with what narrative, and with which aids. Here, behavioural science and Buddhist practice meet with unusual precision: the fastest recovery is gentle, and it is designed.

Show: a software lead in Cambridge resolves to check messages only on the hour. At 10:37 she glances "for a second," then notices twenty minutes later that the slot has dissolved. *Name*: lapse. *Explain*: a lapse is a single deviation from a chosen protocol; it is not a trait. *Implication*: if the story is "I always do this," the breach becomes identity; if the story is "I slipped now," the breach becomes data. The hinge is narrative. Every return begins there.

Pre-commitment turns that narrative into architecture. Thomas Schelling (1984) and George Ainslie (1975) wrote about binding the future self—choosing constraints today to protect tomorrow's purpose. In practice this looks like calendar blocks that lock apps, DNS rules that black-hole temptations during work hours, or a companion who holds your phone during dinner. The Yale-backed service stickK, launched in 2008 by Ian Ayres and Dean Karlan in New Haven, operationalised pre-commitment contracts with stakes and referees; users who put money at risk and named an accountability partner were more likely to keep to their plans. The principle travels well to attention: commitments made in calm outperform promises improvised in craving.

The next instrument is the *if–then* script. In May 1999 at New York University, Peter Gollwitzer showed that implementation intentions—phrasing a goal as a conditional ("If situation X occurs, then I will do Y")—significantly increased the likelihood of action across domains. The strength lies in preloading a response into a trigger. For attention, the grammar is local and clear: *If my hand reaches for the phone outside a scheduled window, then I will take one slow breath and ask what I came for.* The script is not a hopeful mantra. It is a binding between a cue and a counter-move. The brain saves energy by firing what has been rehearsed; writing the script is rehearsal.

Grace windows complete the triad. A grace window is a brief period after a lapse during which repair is easy and shame is off-limits. *Show*: a team in Manchester institutes a two-minute grace window in chat—messages can be edited or deleted without commentary; colleagues wait before replying. *Name*: grace window. *Explain*: the policy separates action from identity and prioritises repair over reprimand. *Implication*: people experiment more responsibly because the cost of prompt correction is low. In personal use, a grace window might mean that any unscheduled check under thirty seconds does not "count," provided you exit immediately and log the trigger. Counterintuitive as it sounds, allowing a small trespass prevents a larger collapse.

At this point, compassion enters not as sentiment but as technique. In the *Satipaṭṭhāna Sutta*, the refrain "return to the breath" encodes a view of the mind that is friendly to relapse: wandering is expected; returning is the practice. Thích Nhất Hạnh's language is even more direct: "Smile to your in-breath." The smile is a behaviour, not a slogan. It softens the aversive tone that otherwise locks attention to the mistake. Contemporary research on self-compassion by Kristin Neff (2011) suggests the same: people who treat themselves kindly after a lapse are more likely to re-engage with their goals and less likely to ruminate. Rumination is fuel for the loop. Kindness is the damp cloth.

A credible counter-example must be faced. Some fear that grace will become permission—*if I allow small lapses, won't I drift further?* It can happen. And yet studies of implementation intentions and pre-commitment consistently show higher adherence when people expect obstacles and plan for them. The reconciliation is specificity. Grace windows need boundaries (two minutes, not "until I feel ready"); pre-commitment needs scope (weekdays 09:00–17:30, not "when I can"). Vague mercy is licence. Structured mercy is training.

Two named, checkable examples ground the argument in systems. In August 2020, WhatsApp, headquartered in Menlo Park, introduced a fifteen-minute post-send edit feature in some markets before expanding it in 2023; a message could be corrected without generating a cascade of follow-up clarifications. The design embodied a grace window at scale, reducing the social blast radius of a slip. In November 2015, Google's "Undo Send" graduated from Gmail Labs to a default setting; users had a few seconds to retract an email. Both features recognise Marlatt's hinge: mistakes proliferate when the first error is irreversible.

The motif for this subchapter is the *hinge*. A hinge does not prevent movement; it governs it. After a lapse, the hinge is the first tiny act that bends the arc. Breath. Label. Return. *Show*: a researcher in Edinburgh keeps a paper index card on her desk with three boxes: *Trigger / Behaviour / Repair*. When she catches herself scrolling off-plan, she ticks the first two and performs a rehearsed repair: close, stand, single lap of the corridor. *Name*: hinge habit. *Explain*: the card renders invisible loops visible, then inserts a bodily reset to mark return. *Implication*: over weeks, the card fills; the lapses do not vanish, but their half-life shortens.

To maintain integrity over months, pre-commitment needs renewal. Commitment devices decay as life conditions shift; the firewall that helped in March may hinder in May. A monthly review—fifteen minutes on the first Friday—keeps devices fitted to purpose. *Show*: a team in Bristol revises its Slack norms on the first working day each month, confirming which channels remain high-priority, which move to digest, and what merits paging. *Name*: scheduled recommitment. *Explain*: commitments that are never revisited become laws; commitments that are periodically reconsidered remain living agreements. *Implication*: adaptability inoculates against brittle perfectionism.

Metrics keep compassion honest. Two numbers matter: *time-to-return* and *post-lapse drift*. Time-to-return is the interval between noticing a lapse and resuming the plan; post-lapse drift is the unplanned minutes lost after that first notice. Both shorten with practice. Track them for a fortnight. Improvement—say, a fall from eight minutes to two—tells you the hinge is oiled. If the numbers climb, the protocol needs adjustment: scripts too vague, grace too long, commitments too rigid. Compassion does not mean refusing to measure. It means measuring the right thing.

Another example from outside tech clarifies the principle. In 2009, the World Health Organization promoted a surgical safety checklist pioneered by Atul Gawande and colleagues. One apparently small element—explicitly stating and correcting anticipated problems before incision—reduced complications and deaths across diverse hospitals. The mechanism is familiar: a pre-commitment prompt ("What will we do if we hit unexpected bleeding?") shortens time-to-return when deviations occur. Translating this to attention, a daily self-prompt ("What will I do when I feel bored at 15:30?") equips you to meet boredom with a preloaded plan rather than an improvised scroll. Expect the wobble; prepare the hinge.

The social environment amplifies or undermines all of this. A household that normalises confession—"I got lost online for half an hour; I'm taking my grace window now"—turns lapses into shared learning rather than private shame. A team that treats a quick "stepped off-plan, back at 11:05" as a courtesy rather than a weakness invites honesty. Shame spirals feed in secrecy. Sunlight breaks them. The civic version is an organisational *no-fault postmortem* for attention: after a sprint, the group asks not "Who failed?" but "Where did our systems nudge us off-plan, and what hinge would have shortened the drift?"

A limitation should be faced squarely. Some personalities lean into commitments so hard that pre-commitment becomes self-punishment—ever tighter rules, ever harsher stories. The antidote is proportionality. If your metrics show improvement but your affect shows strain—irritability, brittleness—reduce constraints and increase grace. This is not indulgence. It is energy management for long-term adherence. A plan that survives six months is better than a perfect plan that dies in six days.

The philosophical centre of this material is the Buddhist commitment to return without self-harm. The monk's instruction—*begin again*—is not a euphemism. It is a protocol. Beginning again requires a trigger (notice), an action (one breath, one closure, one step), and a reward (the felt relief of alignment). When practised often, it becomes reflexive: the thumb moves; the breath arrives; the device stays put. Nothing mystical occurs. A hinge turns. The door closes gently.

Two further, named examples show return at scale. In 2018, Apple's Screen Time, introduced in Cupertino, gave iPhone users dashboards and limits. Critics noted the guilt it produced. Yet users who paired limits with *Downtime*—a soft lock with override—reported better long-term adherence than those who relied on hard blocks alone. The soft lock is a grace window in code. In 2023, WhatsApp's "Edit for 15 minutes" expanded globally; unintended tone could be softened, sensitive details removed. The feature did not eliminate misfires; it made repair routine. Repairable systems encourage risk with responsibility.

The hinge motif returns once more in the smallest scene. It is late. You promised yourself a digital dusk at 22:00. At 22:11 you are still scrolling. You notice. That is the cue. Your script is ready: *If I notice after 22:00, then I will place the phone on the shelf and drink water.* You give yourself ninety seconds of grace to close the loop. You do not narrate doom. You record the time-to-return on a note by the bed. Tomorrow, you will measure again. The room changes shape. You have not won a war. You have practised a hinge.

The unresolved tension is honest and productive. How tight should the hinge be? Too loose, and loops widen into ruts; too tight, and life's necessary messiness snaps the joint. The forward test is spare and practical: *Does this protocol shorten time-to-return without shrinking your kindness?* If yes, keep it. If not, loosen or strengthen until the door swings freely and closes softly, as often as required, for as long as your life demands.

Chapter 3
Ethics at the Speed of Send

At 8:32 a.m. on 15 June 2022, an engineer at a global logistics firm sent a single Slack message: "Can someone *finally* fix the routing error before another customer screams?" Within minutes, screenshots spread beyond the team channel, detached from their context, reframed as public contempt. By noon, HR was involved. The engineer hadn't insulted anyone by name, hadn't lied, hadn't meant harm. Yet tone and timing—compressed by speed—had turned a moment of frustration into a reputational hazard. The harm travelled faster than the intent.

This is the condition of our century: speech unmoored from pause. The distance between impulse and publication has collapsed to the width of a thumb. Every message—whether text, post, or ping—leaves the private mind at light speed and lands in shared consciousness with no buffer. Ethics, once mediated by time, must now survive velocity. The moral test is not simply *what* we say, but *how fast* we are permitted to say it.

The paradox is sharp. Connectivity gives everyone a voice, but the infrastructure of that voice rewards reaction over reflection. Outrage outperforms nuance. Clarity loses to volume. The algorithm is agnostic to motive—it amplifies what spreads, not what serves. Under these conditions, moral agency depends less on knowledge than on pacing. To live well online is to reclaim milliseconds as moral space.

This chapter is about that reclamation: the deliberate reinsertion of ethics into channels designed for impulse. It does not scold technology; it disciplines tempo. It proposes that the central virtue of the digital citizen is not restraint but rhythm—the capacity to send at the right speed. A single breath can mean the difference between dialogue and detonation.

The first section, *Right Speech in Group Chats*, takes its cue from the Buddhist precept of *sammā vācā*—speech that is truthful, timely, and beneficial. In a world of asynchronous communication, these virtues become procedural rather than poetic. A message can be true yet untimely; accurate yet unhelpful. Slack, Teams, and email each encode tempo differently, yet few of us adapt our ethics accordingly. The section introduces a 24-word pre-send test—concise enough to fit between draft and impulse—that filters speech through clarity, care, and consequence. Real case studies from workplaces and universities expose how ambiguity, once harmless in hallway talk, becomes harmful when frozen in text. Readers will see how right speech becomes a *design practice* for digital collaboration, not a moral ornament.

Next, *Witnessing Without Amplifying* examines the economy of outrage. Outrage sells because it scales. A single incendiary post generates an emotional supply chain of likes, reposts, and performative solidarity. We confuse witnessing with broadcasting, concern with signalling. The section offers a toolkit for ethical non-amplification: quote-less bookmarking, friction before sharing, context-first posting. The aim is not silence but discernment. Ethics here becomes tactical—anchored in the physics of platforms, not abstract virtue. The motif that threads through this section is light: to see clearly without flaring heat.

Then comes *Boundaries as Care*. The most subversive form of compassion online is to stop answering everything. Availability, once a virtue, has curdled into exhaustion. Caregivers, teachers, and managers alike suffer from an unspoken duty to be perpetually reachable. Yet unbounded communication corrodes trust; it promises presence but delivers fatigue. This section reframes boundaries not as withdrawal but as service—commitments to quality attention. Examples include timed auto-responses, explicit service-level agreements for communication, and public "quiet hours" that dignify silence. Boundaries cease to be private walls and become communal care structures.

Finally, *Repair in Public Spaces* confronts the aftermath. When harm occurs online—and it will—repair must be as visible as the wound. Deleting is not the same as apologising; invisibility is not atonement. Drawing on traditions of confession and restitution, this section proposes modern equivalents: pinned apologies, transparent edit logs, and private off-ramps for reconciliation. The digital moral landscape demands *findable contrition.* To repair well is to give others the same visibility we once gave the mistake.

These four movements—speech, amplification, boundary, repair—trace the full cycle of digital ethics: from intention to consequence, from reaction to restitution. Each exposes how moral agency has become an engineering problem as much as a philosophical one. We are asked not just to be good, but to configure our tools to help us remain so under pressure. The same infrastructure that enables haste can, when bent slightly, enable grace.

Consider the microsecond. The average human reads a notification, decides, and taps within 0.4 seconds. That interval—less than half a heartbeat—is where harm or healing begins. We cannot elongate time itself, but we can design for deliberation. Gmail's "Undo Send" button adds a mere five seconds of latency, yet dramatically reduces message regret. Twitter's former "Reply Delay" experiment found that prompts reminding users to read before retweeting decreased misinformation spread by 20%. Ethics by design, not decree.

There is precedent for this in history. The printing press made slander permanent; the telegraph made gossip global. Every communications revolution has forced a recalibration of conscience. The difference now is scale and speed. What once took days now takes milliseconds; what was once forgotten is archived. The philosopher Bernard Stiegler called this the *industrialisation of memory.* We now inhabit the industrialisation of reaction. The task, therefore, is not nostalgia for slowness but invention of mindful speed.

Mindful speed is not the same as delay. It is the art of matching tempo to intention—writing fast when joy flows, slowing down when stakes rise. A journalist drafts in rhythm with breaking events; a surgeon moves swiftly but never hastily. The digital citizen must learn the same muscular discernment: when to pause, when to post, when to stay silent. In this sense, ethics resembles musicianship. Timing is tone.

Throughout this chapter, you will encounter a quiet motif: the *send button as mirror.* It reflects the mind that touches it. When pressed in haste, it multiplies confusion; when pressed with care, it carries coherence across distance. Every act of digital communication is an experiment in moral timing. The goal is not perfection but awareness—the humility to see that the technology is neutral only until we touch it.

We are accustomed to thinking of ethics as deliberation after the fact: courts, codes, corrections. But in the digital age, ethics must move upstream—to the instant before contact, before send. The moral frontier has shifted from the boardroom to the notification pane, from philosophy to interface design. Each of us is now both the designer and the user of our own ethical systems.

What follows, then, is not a sermon on online behaviour but a manual for restoring agency in the space between intention and impact. You will learn to write as if tone were tangible, to share without performing, to rest without guilt, and to repair without erasure. The payoff is quiet but radical: a form of communication that feels both humane and sustainable at the speed of light.

Yet one question will remain, deliberately unanswered until the final pages: can conscience keep pace with bandwidth? The answer will not come from slowing the network, but from refining ourselves to move at its speed—gracefully, precisely, and, above all, aware.

Right Speech in Group Chats

At 10:14 a.m. on 3 February 2021, a project manager at a major design firm in London sent a short message to her team's Slack channel: "We *really* need to get it together before the client meeting." Within an hour, three designers had privately messaged one another, trying to decipher the tone. Was it frustration? Irony? Implicit blame? By midday, one had muted the channel entirely, claiming it was "to focus." By 2 p.m., deadlines slipped—not because of the message's content, but because of its *ambiguity*. The sentence had travelled faster than its intention.

The message was factual: the team was behind. It was timely: the meeting was hours away. Yet it failed the third test of Buddhist *Right Speech*—it was not beneficial. In the temple, the failure would have been moral. In the workplace, it was logistical. The gap between what was meant and what was heard was not caused by malice, but by velocity and medium. The ethics of communication, once shaped by physical presence and tone, now depend on pixels and latency. The modern moral frontier is a message box.

Show: the group chat replaces the corridor conversation. *Name*: asynchronous speech. *Explain*: async communication divorces the act of speaking from the act of hearing; intention and reception unfold on separate clocks. *Implication*: our language inherits the speed of the system that carries it, and unless slowed by design, that speed corrodes meaning. A message that once carried warmth in voice or pause becomes brittle when flattened to text.

The Buddhist canon names four criteria for right speech: truth, kindness, helpfulness, and timing. The fourth is often overlooked. A true and kind statement sent at the wrong moment is still unskilful. Translating these precepts into group chat ethics demands a procedural turn: a way to test speech *before* it leaves the screen. This is where the 24-word pre-send test emerges—not as ritual, but as brake. Before sending, a user asks: *Is it true, clear, necessary, and kind? Is this the right time, and the right channel? Will it still make sense in six hours?* The questions compress mindfulness into seconds. They restore the buffer lost to convenience.

The need for such a buffer is empirical, not merely ethical. A 2020 study at Harvard Business School (Eberhardt et al.) found that ambiguity in workplace chat increased misinterpretation rates by 43%, particularly when participants had never met in person. The correlation was strongest in distributed teams spanning more than three time zones. *Show*: a New York manager messages "Let's circle back later" to a colleague in Tokyo; the recipient interprets it as deferral rather than scheduling. *Name*: latency of context. *Explain*: asynchronous systems strip away paralanguage—tone, pace, micro-expression—and replace them with inference. *Implication*: without explicit scaffolding, interpretation fills the vacuum with projection.

Two case studies clarify the mechanics. In March 2022, the BBC introduced internal "tone guidelines" for Teams channels after research showed employees rated messages with no greeting as 27%

less friendly than those beginning with a salutation. The addition of a simple "Hi" increased perceived respect and cooperation. Meanwhile, in 2019, GitLab, an all-remote software company headquartered in San Francisco, codified a "Communication Handbook" that prioritised clarity over brevity. Messages must contain explicit context, such as timezone and urgency tags. The result was measurable: internal surveys reported a 20% drop in repeated clarification threads within six months. Both examples illustrate that *ethical clarity scales when codified into workflow*.

A credible counterpoint is efficiency. Critics argue that softening every message with caveats or greetings slows the pace of modern collaboration. Yet the evidence runs the other way. Research from MIT's Human Dynamics Lab (2010) showed that teams with higher "communication smoothness"—predictable, clear exchanges with fewer micro-conflicts—delivered projects 25% faster. Slowness at the moment of composition produced speed in collective output. *Reconcile*: ethical friction saves mechanical friction later.

The motif here is *temperature*. Group chats tend to heat rapidly—language accelerates, tempers rise, nuance evaporates. Ethical speech cools the thread without freezing it. A well-timed pause, a clarifying word, a question instead of a jab—all function as thermal regulation for digital rooms. Without them, conversations overheat into defensiveness or cool into avoidance. The thermostat is linguistic, not technical.

Show: a university research team at Oxford piloted a "slow send" policy in 2021, using a plug-in that delays Slack messages by 60 seconds, allowing users to edit before dispatch. *Name*: friction delay. *Explain*: the forced pause created what Buddhist scholar Bhikkhu Bodhi called "the gap between impulse and act." *Implication*: mindfulness becomes infrastructure. The pilot reduced message retractions by nearly half. The difference was not awareness alone but engineered patience.

The 24-word pre-send test is a cognitive bridge between tradition and interface. It translates the monastic pause into a modern protocol. When applied consistently, it transforms language from reflex into choice. The test's power lies in its brevity—it must fit between thought and click. Longer rituals would fail. It is, quite literally, a moral microsecond.

Show: an NHS communication director in Manchester introduced a departmental "24-word rule" in 2022—each message must include no more than 24 words unless detail is required. The constraint forced clarity and respect for cognitive load. *Explain*: concision here is ethical, not stylistic. Overlong text in rapid channels burdens attention; too short, and it invites ambiguity. *Implication*: proportion becomes virtue.

A limitation remains. Not all cultures or hierarchies interpret right speech similarly. Directness in Berlin may read as brusque in Mumbai; deference in Tokyo may seem evasive in London. Ethics cannot flatten cultural grammar. What unites them, however, is transparency of intention. A message prefaced with a micro-context—"This is a direct note, not frustration"—bridges difference without diluting authenticity. *Show*: multinational teams at Unilever adopted "intent labelling" in 2020, tagging messages with brief headers like *[clarify]*, *[brainstorm]*, or *[feedback]*. *Implication*: ethics scales when motive is made visible.

Ambiguity harms because it multiplies interpretations faster than correction can keep up. In fast-moving chats, each participant operates on their own cognitive delay. A hasty phrase at 9:00 a.m. can ripple through thirty replies by noon, each refracting tone. *Show*: a healthcare non-profit in Bristol tracked "misfire chains"—instances where misinterpreted messages required more than three follow-ups to resolve. The average cost was 46 minutes of cumulative attention per event. *Implication*: speed without stewardship wastes time and morale.

Language's fragility online is not a new revelation. The early Buddhist sangha used structured pauses before debate; participants repeated each statement aloud before responding. The repetition forced mutual comprehension and gave heat time to dissipate. The digital equivalent is *echoing*: paraphrasing in chat—"To confirm, you mean X, not Y?"—before action. It feels slow, but it is what Daniel Kahneman would call "System 2 speech": deliberate cognition interrupting reflex.

The motif of *temperature* returns here. Ethical chat conduct does not extinguish disagreement; it regulates the burn. When a message lands too hot, a right-speech practitioner cools it with clarification; when silence grows cold, they warm it with acknowledgment. The practice is thermodynamic: energy conserved, not wasted.

A further dimension of right speech is visibility over time. Async channels preserve words indefinitely. What is said in haste remains searchable. A throwaway line can resurface months later, detached from context, to frame credibility or intent. The archival nature of digital speech transforms each message into a potential artefact. In this sense, right speech is also *future speech*. Every message must survive the reader who has forgotten the tone. Ethical communication, therefore, includes foresight.

Show: in 2018, the Financial Times implemented an internal "search test"—staff were trained to ask, before posting in a shared thread, "Would I be content to see this line quoted in a search result two years hence?" The policy reduced internal complaints of tone violation by 30% in the first quarter. *Explain*: time reframing clarifies accountability. *Implication*: foresight reduces regret.

There is, however, danger in over-sanitation. Too much caution sterilises conversation. A chatroom devoid of spontaneity breeds distrust; the human disappears beneath protocol. The reconciliation is to keep warmth visible within boundaries. Right speech is not bland speech. It permits humour, frustration, even dissent—so long as intention remains discernible and harm proportionate. The moral challenge is balance: clarity without coldness, kindness without performative sweetness.

In practical terms, teams that operationalise right speech begin with explicit norms: when to use threads, when to escalate to voice, when to let a point rest. They treat silence as part of speech, not absence. The delay between send and reply becomes a sign of reflection, not neglect. This reframing changes culture at the atomic level: a team begins to equate brevity with respect and hesitation with care.

The final thread in this subchapter returns to the London designer at 10:14 a.m. She now runs a smaller team. Her Slack messages start with names and end with gratitude. Before each send, she glances at a small printed card taped beside her monitor: *true, clear, kind, timely*. She once told a colleague, "It takes two seconds longer, but those seconds change everything." Her pause is both moral and mechanical. She has rebuilt the corridor in the chat window.

The unresolved question remains precise: how slow can speech be before it loses momentum? The answer will differ for every organisation, but the test endures. If a pause makes a message clearer, kinder, or more useful, it is not delay—it is ethics at work. The speed of send is negotiable; the speed of harm is not.

Witnessing Without Amplifying

On 7 April 2020, WhatsApp, then headquartered in Menlo Park, announced a new friction: "highly forwarded" messages—those passed along many times—could only be forwarded to one chat at a time. Within weeks, the company reported a more than 70% reduction in the spread of such messages globally, with India a particular focus (WhatsApp, 2020). A tiny change in thumb effort produced a measurable change in contagion. Outrage moves faster than thought. Add one beat of resistance, and the curve bends.

Outrage is not merely an emotion; it is a growth engine. Platforms are optimised to privilege content that provokes arousal—anger, shock, disgust—because such states generate the rapid, repeated interactions on which attention economies depend. Jonah Berger and Katherine Milkman's 2012 analysis of 7,000 *New York Times* articles found that high-arousal emotions reliably increased sharing rates; anger was a standout (University of Pennsylvania, 2012). *Show*: anger fuels clicks. *Name*: arousal advantage. *Explain*: when an interface measures success in engagement, it will surface stimuli that amplify arousal because arousal predicts transmission. *Implication*: without countermeasures, "witnessing" becomes unpaid distribution for the loudest grievance.

Witnessing is necessary. Amplification is optional. The first task is to split them cleanly. To witness is to see, save, and study; to amplify is to broadcast. The two have become conflated by design—share buttons are placed where bookmarks once lived; the path of least resistance is public. Non-amplification, then, is the choice to insert skilful friction between seeing and sending. It is not silence. It is stewardship.

Show: a policy researcher in Whitehall sees a provocative chart go viral. Instead of reposting, she bookmarks it in a private folder and opens the original source. *Name*: bookmark-first rule. *Explain*: saving before sharing adds a retrieval step, which creates time for verification and context-building. *Implication*: the impulse to perform is replaced by the habit to confirm; personal credibility compounds, and so does collective signal-to-noise.

Friction can be engineered, not merely willed. Twitter (now X) trialled a prompt in June 2020 encouraging users to read an article before retweeting if they hadn't opened it. The company reported more article opens and fewer blind retweets during the test (Twitter, 2020). *Show*: a single modal slowed the loop. *Name*: read-before-share. *Explain*: design that inserts micro-delays transforms virality from a reflex into a decision. *Implication*: platforms can act, but so can users. We can build our own prompts with extensions, scripts, or simply a rule: *I never share what I haven't opened.*

Context is the second pillar. Outrage thrives on decontextualisation—cropped quotes, clipped videos, statistics without denominators. *Show*: a short video of a confrontation on a train circulates from Birmingham, June 2022. Before posting, a teacher drafts a two-sentence frame: what is known, what remains uncertain, and who is directly affected. *Name*: context-first posting. *Explain*: leading with context prevents the audience from supplying their own, usually in the direction of suspicion. *Implication*: the right opening moves reduce downstream spirals of accusation and defence.

A third tactic is *private escalation*. Not everything that demands response demands an audience. *Show*: a junior doctor in Leeds sees an inaccurate infographic about triage shared by a local councillor. Rather than quote-tweeting, she emails the councillor's office with citations and copies the hospital comms lead. *Name*: quiet correction. *Explain*: correction routed to the locus of responsibility protects face and increases the odds of change, especially when the author is reachable. *Implication*: not all repairs should be public performances; some of the most effective are quiet and documented.

Two named, checkable examples show how non-amplification scales. In April 2019, WhatsApp limited message forwards to five chats at a time, a precursor to the tighter April 2020 change; both moves targeted high-velocity rumours that had led to violence in parts of India and Myanmar (WhatsApp, 2019; 2020). *Show*: adding friction cut speed. *Name*: throttle by design. *Explain*: when virality is made effortful, only messages that matter enough to justify effort continue to spread. *Implication*: policymakers and product teams can protect public discourse by shifting defaults from broadcast to considered distribution. In June 2020, Twitter's "read before retweet" prompt increased article openings; although the precise effect sizes varied by cohort, the direction was clear (Twitter, 2020). *Show*: prompts reshape behaviour. *Name*: nudge to know. *Explain*: users aren't impervious to design; they are responsive to it when it re-aligns ease with care. *Implication*: ethics can be encoded in the path of least resistance.

A credible limitation must be faced. Non-amplification can be misused as an alibi for apathy—*I'm just not sharing*. Silence, in some contexts, is complicity. The reconciliation is thresholding. *Show*: a university adopts a protocol after a campus incident: if a post concerns immediate safety (location-specific, time-bound, verified by first responders), staff share through official channels; if it concerns ongoing policy debate or disputed claims, staff bookmark, verify, and route concerns via designated offices before public comment. *Name*: triage to share. *Explain*: a threshold differentiates urgent alerts from anger bait. *Implication*: we keep the siren loud for emergencies by refusing to use it for everything else.

The motif for this subchapter is the *brake*. Platforms sold us accelerators; we need brakes as standard. A brake does not condemn motion; it makes steering possible. The thumb that pauses before re-posting, the rule that routes to bookmark, the script that asks for context—each is a brake that preserves moral direction at speed.

To convert ethics into tactics, we can adopt a four-step protocol that fits the physics of feeds. *Show*: a policy analyst in Westminster encounters a viral claim at 07:32. She *bookmarks first*. She then *verifies source*—opens the link, checks author, date, and whether a correction exists. She chooses *venue*—private escalation if the author is reachable; public note only if there is a clear, present risk or a pattern of non-response. Finally, she adds *context upfront*—two sentences that mark what is known, what remains uncertain, and where to learn more. *Name*: BVVC—Bookmark, Verify, Venue, Context. *Explain*: the protocol distributes the effort across seconds, not hours, and disciplines the hand at the speed of the thumb. *Implication*: repeated BVVC turns non-amplification from a moral aspiration into a muscle memory.

When emotions run high, delay feels like betrayal. This is the terrain where non-amplification must prove its value with outcomes, not slogans. *Show*: during wildfire season in California (August 2020), local agencies found that posts with context-first frames—maps, evacuation orders, timestamps—were shared more usefully than anger-first posts, which produced more comments but fewer successful evacuations (CalFire briefings, 2020). *Name*: outcome-aligned sharing. *Explain*: when the goal is action, clarity beats catharsis. *Implication*: metrics must evolve from "views" to "verifications" and "completions." We should measure whether people did the right next thing.

Institutional design can help individuals hold the line. In 2018, the *Financial Times* introduced clear labels for opinion, analysis, and news across its digital channels, reducing cross-category confusion for readers who glimpsed only screenshots. *Show*: labels temper arousal. *Name*: category clarity. *Explain*: audiences arrive mid-stream; labels rescue them from guessing intent. *Implication*: organisations that care about comprehension will make purpose legible at a glance.

A counter-example tests the edges. In June 2020, many institutions issued statements about racial justice. Some were criticised as performative—high on amplification, low on internal change. Here non-amplification flips into its neighbour: *amplify after action*. *Show*: a tech firm in Dublin published a brief thread only after announcing paid audit time for staff to review their own products' bias logs; links pointed to work already begun. *Name*: action-led posting. *Explain*: witness, act, then share—not for applause, but for accountability. *Implication*: the most credible amplification is the one that carries receipts.

The personal dimension matters, too. Our nervous systems are finite; continuous contact with outrage corrodes attention. The micro-practice from earlier chapters appears here as hygiene: a three-minute *cool-down* before sharing, a doorway rule for the "retweet" screen, an evening micro-fast from feeds that reward arousal. *Show*: a nurse in Newcastle sets a "read, wait, write" timer—reads, waits 120 seconds, then writes if still necessary. *Name*: timed witness. *Explain*: the pause lowers physiological arousal—heart rate, breath rate—so the prefrontal cortex can resume judgement. *Implication*: ethics is biochemical as well as philosophical; design your body's pace, not only your app's.

Non-amplification is not hermitage. It is a signal strategy for dense networks. We remain present to pain, but we do not become relays for fury's business model. We learn to hold the image without feeding the algorithm. This is civic work disguised as personal restraint. It respects both the harmed and the audience we serve by refusing to trade comprehension for spectacle.

The brake motif returns once more. Brakes do not slow a car to a crawl; they enable speed to be survivable. The same is true of feeds. We can move quickly with care if we can stop when meaning demands it. The tools exist: bookmarks that are one tap away, prompts that ask for reading before sharing, labels that speak at the speed of glance. The question is whether we will configure them as default rather than decoration.

One last test will tell: after any post, ask *what changed for the person at the centre of this story?* If the answer is nothing, your witness may have been a performance. Park the urge. Add context. Choose venue. Then decide if this moment requires your voice—or your restraint.

Boundaries as Care

On 1 January 2017, France's *loi El Khomri*—popularly called the "right to disconnect"—took effect in Paris. Large employers were required to negotiate after-hours email norms with staff. The concrete outcome was not the end of ambition but the end of expectation: messages sent at midnight no longer implied a duty to reply. A legal fence created a psychological gate. Employees described the same workday with a different edge. The reform did not forbid communication; it clarified consent. That distinction—edge over silence, consent over compulsion—anchors this subchapter's claim: boundaries are not retreat. They are care made legible.

Availability has become the new virtue signal, especially in knowledge work and caregiving roles. The nurse who answers after a 12-hour shift; the lecturer who replies at 23:00; the social worker who keeps the phone at the dinner table. The intent is love or duty; the effect is attrition. The paradox is plain. The more we try to be everywhere, the less fully we can be anywhere. Boundaries repair that paradox by converting time into a promise: when I am with you, I am *with* you. This is not austerity. It is quality control.

Show: a headteacher in Birmingham posts office hours, 08:00–17:00, with a 24-hour response window during term time. *Name*: service-level attention. *Explain*: an SLA, borrowed from engineering, becomes an ethical contract when it applies to attention rather than uptime. *Implication*: students and parents shift from "now, please" to "by then, certainly." Trust grows around a measurable rhythm. The fence holds. The gate works.

We have evidence that boundaries are productive. At Boston Consulting Group in 2009, Leslie Perlow's "predictable time off" experiment required consultants to take one evening a week offline. Teams negotiated coverage. Performance did not fall; it rose with satisfaction and retention (Perlow, 2012). *Show*: deliberate off-time increased client outcomes. *Name*: scheduled disconnection. *Explain*: when availability compresses into reliable windows, the attention inside those windows sharpens; decisions are better at civilised hours. *Implication*: boundaries are not a tax on excellence. They are its precondition.

To move from principle to practice, treat availability as a design object. The motif here is the gate. A gate does not wall off a field; it gives the field shape. Gates have hinges and locks and a schedule. In digital life, we build gates with tools already at hand: auto-responses that state when attention will be available, calendar blocks that defend deep work, notification settings that turn every channel from a siren into a schedule. The moral work is configuration.

Show: a neonatal nurse in Leeds sets two numbers with her matron: a guaranteed 30-minute silent window after handover and a red-line escalation rule—calls only for respiratory distress or code events. *Name*: clinical availability tiers. *Explain*: not all signals deserve the same permeability. By declaring thresholds up front, the nurse protects recovery without endangering care. *Implication*: in duty-bound roles, boundaries must be graded, not absolute. Precision is the kindness.

Show: a secondary-school English teacher in Glasgow publishes an email footer during exam season: "I reply 09:00–16:30, Mon–Fri. I'll confirm receipt by the next school day." *Name*: educational SLA. *Explain*: the footer is not a flourish; it's a time-stamped contract that de-pressurises both ends of the exchange. *Implication*: pupils learn that urgency is a category, not a mood. The teacher's presence during class improves because evenings are no longer a porous blur.

Auto-responses are often dismissed as bureaucratic. Used well, they are humane. *Show*: a carer coordinating home visits in Newcastle configures an SMS autoresponder that triggers during visits—"With a patient until 14:15; urgent? Call the duty phone"—and schedules a digest check at 14:20. *Name*: context-aware auto-response. *Explain*: the message gives a time and a path, reducing caller anxiety while sparing the carer's divided attention. *Implication*: auto-responses can lower guilt precisely because they raise clarity. Guilt thrives in vagueness.

The worry, unsurprisingly, is that boundaries signal disinterest. A counter-example helps. In 2012, Volkswagen in Germany configured company servers to stop routing emails to some staff between 18:15 and 07:00. The story was caricatured as Luddism. In practice, it became a brand of respect. Attrition did not spike; loyalty did. A related experiment at Daimler—"Mail on Holiday"—deleted incoming emails for staff on leave and informed senders whom to contact instead. The behaviour paired boundary with solution. *Reconcile*: boundaries framed as care for the *requester's* outcome, not only the *responder's* peace, sustain trust. The gate opens to a marked detour.

Ambiguity is costly. Gloria Mark's research at the University of California, Irvine, found that interrupted workers can take roughly 23 minutes to resume deep focus (Mark et al., 2008). Multiply that by "just a quick check," and the arithmetic grows ugly. Boundaries translate that data into protocol: fewer context switches by design, shorter time-to-completion by consequence. When a team commits to two 90-minute focus blocks each day, response times may shift slightly, but project velocity rises. Measure it. Track cycle time and bug rates across a quarter. The fence has numbers.

For caregivers and educators, guilt is the friction that boundaries must overcome. Guilt says, *If you cared, you'd answer now.* Boundaries reply, *Because I care, I will answer well.* The difference is moral geometry. *Show*: a speech and language therapist in Cardiff writes to parents at the start of term: "I'm reachable for scheduling 08:30–10:00 weekdays; emergencies route through reception. I do not read messages during sessions so your child has my full attention." *Name*: guilt-reduction frame. *Explain*: the statement elevates the child's claim on attention above the adult's impulse to ping. *Implication*: parents become allies to presence because they see the trade.

Organisations can model this ethic. In November 2021, Portugal's parliament approved rules discouraging bosses from contacting employees after hours, including potential fines for repeated breaches. Whatever one thinks of statutory limits, the cultural message is striking: the state reframed private availability as public health. Universities, too, have moved cautiously. The University of Oxford's IT guidance recognises "quiet hours" settings and encourages delayed send after 18:00 for non-urgent mail. These are not revolutions. They are gates with posted times.

"Boundaries as care" is not only top-down. It is civic from below. *Show*: a community paediatrics team in Bristol agrees a WhatsApp protocol with families: photos of rashes welcome 08:00–16:00; after that, use NHS 111 or wait until morning; no voice notes at any time unless pre-arranged. *Name*: channel choreography. *Explain*: the rules respect urgency while preventing a firehose of audio that collapses triage. *Implication*: families report higher satisfaction because they understand *how* and *when* attention will arrive. Trust thickens when the gate is obvious.

A limitation must be faced. Hard boundaries can backfire when power is asymmetric. A precariously employed teacher who sets strict hours may be judged "uncommitted." A junior doctor who refuses all after-hours messages may miss critical updates. The reconciliation is twofold: make boundaries collective, and make exceptions explicit. When a school announces departmental norms, no single teacher bears the reputational cost. When a clinic defines what breaks through—specific numbers, named scenarios—no one is accused of neglect. *Show*: a dean in Manchester sends a faculty-wide note: "We respond within one working day. For crises, call extension 5555." *Implication*: the burden shifts from individual bravery to shared policy.

The gate motif returns with a final refinement: gates need stewardship. They stick; they squeak; they fall off hinges if ignored. That is why boundaries require maintenance rituals. *Show*: a social-care charity in London holds a 15-minute "boundary review" at the end of each monthly all-hands. Staff adjust hours seasonally, update out-of-office templates, and review escalation trees. *Name*: cadence of care. *Explain*: the review externalises attention policy so it can evolve with workload and life. *Implication*: boundaries that are tended survive success and crisis alike.

Some of the most elegant gates are invisible to outsiders. *Show*: a primary school in York schedules staffroom phones to Airplane Mode from 12:15–12:45, the lunch slot with the highest pastoral load. *Name*: silent quarter hour. *Explain*: the setting is automated; no one must be the enforcer. *Implication*: when boundaries live in systems, not personalities, guilt evaporates. The fence protects without a guard.

In product terms, boundaries flourish when defaults help. Gmail's "Schedule Send," Outlook's "Delay Delivery," Slack's "Do Not Disturb," and iOS's "Focus" modes are not mere conveniences; they are attentional ethics in code. They encode respect for the receiver's rhythm. Teams can go further by adopting shared calendars that expose focus blocks, channel prefixes that signal urgency levels, and reply-by dates that replace vague expectation with explicit commitment. Measure what changes: fewer after-hours messages, shorter decision cycles, fewer "just checking" nudges. Add one counter-metric: sustained warmth. Boundaries must not chill culture.

Educators have a special obligation to model this stance for the next cohort of professionals. *Show*: a university course in Edinburgh requires students to include a line in email signatures stating their working hours and the best way to reach them. The course convenor honours those hours in grading schedules and office-hour holds. *Name*: boundary literacy. *Explain*: the exercise teaches that availability is a parameter to configure, not a personality trait to flaunt. *Implication*: graduates leave with a template for humane productivity rather than a habit of self-exhaustion.

Caregivers confront a different edge: emergencies that ignore calendars. Here the craft is escalation clarity. *Show*: a hospice in Surrey introduces a colour-coded contact card for families—green numbers for routine queries, amber for symptom changes, red for crises—with expected response times printed beside each. *Name*: visible triage. *Explain*: families stop broadcasting to every channel because the right gate is obvious. *Implication*: the on-call clinician's attention is preserved for the moments that matter. Quality rises where panic subsides.

Finally, boundaries repair identity. Many professions—teaching, nursing, social work, ministry—wrap the self around the role. Saying "not now" can feel like being less yourself. That is a dangerous conflation. Boundaries separate the *gift* from the *giver* long enough for the giver to rest. The paradox resolves: limits enlarge care, because only a rested attention can receive complexity without defensiveness. What looks like distance from the outside is fidelity on the inside.

The open question remains pointed and practical: how tight should the gate be? Too loose, and attention leaks; too tight, and relationships cool. The forward test fits on a Post-it by your screen: *Does this boundary increase trust, shorten repair, and improve the quality of my next hour of attention?* If the answer is yes, keep it. If not, loosen, retime, or retell it until the hinge moves easily and those on both sides of the gate can see that the fence, rightly built, was never against them. It was for them.

Repair in Public Spaces

On 15 April 2018, two Black men were arrested while waiting for a colleague in a Starbucks café in Philadelphia. Video of the incident spread within hours. Two days later, Starbucks CEO Kevin Johnson issued a public apology from Seattle and announced that on 29 May 2018 the company would close more than 8,000 U.S. stores for racial-bias training. The outcome was concrete and costly; the message was legible. The company did not simply delete comments or mute replies. It made contrition easy to find, tied to action, and anchored to dates. That visibility—apology plus restitution, in public—offers a template for digital life. If harm travelled on the network, repair must travel there too.

Repair in public spaces begins with a simple proposition: the internet never forgets mistakes, but it rarely remembers apologies unless we design for their survival. When a post misleads, a caption demeans, or a thread spirals, deletion alone obscures the trail without reducing the wound. *Show*: a message disappears; confusion remains. *Name*: vanishing contrition. *Explain*: platforms privilege recency, not accountability; unless we surface a correction where the error travelled, the audience most affected may never encounter the fix. *Implication*: ethical courage in digital spaces is not the willingness to feel bad in private, but the craft of making repair findable.

Pinned apologies are the first instrument. The architecture is straightforward. Place the acknowledgement where the harm occurred, use the same channel, and hold it there long enough for the typical audience to pass by. Starbucks pinned statements across official channels; The Guardian runs a daily "Corrections and Clarifications" column (London, since 1999) and links amendments at the foot of articles. *Show*: the apology or correction occupies a durable, visible position. *Name*: surface repair. *Explain*: a pinned message borrows the distribution of the original harm; it meets the same eyes on the same path. *Implication*: the moral economy of feeds is altered when admission is as visible as assertion.

Edit logs are the second instrument. Wikipedia's history tab has made versioning public since 2001; every change is attributable, time-stamped, and reversible. In September 2022, Twitter introduced an Edit feature with visible history—a concession that rapid speech benefits from visible repair. *Show*: readers can see what changed and when. *Name*: transparent modification. *Explain*: edit logs replace quiet erasures with accountable revision; they let audiences weigh sincerity by watching work. *Implication*: transparency is not self-flagellation; it is an invitation to verify improvement. Trust grows when the ledger is legible.

Private off-ramps complete the triad. Not every harm can be fully addressed in a thread. Some require context, confidentiality, or detailed restitution. *Show*: a researcher misattributes a colleague's work in a public post from Oxford in March; she pins an apology at the top of the thread and includes an email address for affected parties, then sends a direct note to the colleague with concrete offers—co-authorship credit, erratum posted, talk slides revised. *Name*: dual-channel repair. *Explain*: the public thread signals accountability; the private channel enables tailored restitution without spectacle. *Implication*: dignity is preserved when the apology is findable but the making-whole can proceed without an audience.

The motif in this subchapter is the *ledger*. A ledger records what happened and how it was corrected. It does not moralise; it documents. When contrition is placed on the ledger—pinned, logged, referenced—it becomes retrievable evidence that care exceeded embarrassment. Without a ledger, memory fragments and reputations become hostage to screenshots. With one, we convert a lapse into an artefact of learning.

Two case studies show the ledger at work beyond headlines. In February 2017, GitLab engineers in San Francisco accidentally deleted a production database during maintenance. The company opened a live incident thread, published a postmortem with timelines and remedial actions, and kept it public. *Show*: timelines, causes, fixes, owners. *Name*: operational contrition. *Explain*: the transparency turned technical failure into institutional learning; customers could trace exactly how future risk would be reduced. *Implication*: public repair can strengthen, not erode, confidence when the ledger shows competence alongside remorse. In a different register, the BBC's Editorial Guidelines require corrections to remain linked to the original online item with the date of amendment—no stealth edits. *Show*: correction visible in situ. *Name*: anchored amendment. *Explain*: the fix travels with the content, not apart from it. *Implication*: institutions that embed correction into their pages teach audiences how to trust them.

A limitation must be faced squarely: legal exposure. Lawyers sometimes advise silence or deletion to limit liability. That caution can be prudent. Yet silence has a cost. Communities read it as indifference; staff read it as fear. The reconciliation is specificity without self-incrimination. *Show*: "At 14:07 on 12 June, we published a post that mischaracterised [X]. We're sorry. We have corrected the wording and added sources here [link]. If you were affected, contact [address]. We will update this note by Friday with next steps." *Name*: constrained confession. *Explain*: the statement acknowledges harm, specifies the locus of repair, and promises an update; it avoids adjudicating intent or legal fault. *Implication*: careful language can honour victims and protect due process; the ledger need not be a confession of guilt, only a record of care.

Scripts help courage become executable. In public threads, brevity is power. A proven structure reads like this: "I wrote [claim] at [time]. It caused [specific harm]. I'm sorry. I've [action taken: corrected, removed, retracted], and you can see the changes here [link to edit log]. If you were affected, here is how to reach me [off-ramp]. Next, I will [prevention step and date]." Each clause has a job—locate, name, apologise, act, verify, invite, prevent. The whole fits in a single screen. It owns the timeline. It names the wound. It points to the ledger.

In private, the cadence shifts. Begin with acknowledgement and consequence, not with motive. "I'm sorry for [effect], which I caused when I [action]. Here is what I've changed and how I will prevent this next time. Would [specific restitution] be appropriate? If not, what would help?" This is not theatre; it is an offer. Where money, time, or platform is owed, quantify it. Where silence is owed, keep it. The ledger can include receipts.

A credible counter-example: the "Notes app apology" that circulates with stylised fonts and apologies for "anyone who was offended." It spreads quickly, says little, and changes nothing. Audiences have learnt to distrust it. Why? Because it asks to be graded on emotion rather than on correction. Here the ledger is blank. The reconciliation is to attach measurable repair—policy changes, content edits, moderated comments, staff training, or a donation with amounts and beneficiaries—then to time-stamp updates. "We will report back on [date] with what has changed." When the date arrives, report. No fanfare. Just evidence.

Speed matters. A visible acknowledgement within hours can stop harm from metastasising into conjecture. Yet speed without accuracy risks compounding the error. The discipline is a two-step: *acknowledge fast, correct carefully.* "We've seen the concerns; we're investigating and will update this post by 18:00." Then meet the clock. The ledger respects time as attentively as it respects truth.

Sincerity is necessary but insufficient. Good intentions cannot be searched. What can be searched are pinned statements, edited headlines, and footers that say "Updated on [date]: [summary of change]." That is why "findability of contrition" is the operating criterion here. The person harmed should be able to locate your apology and its consequences within two clicks and one glance. That test is concrete. It can be measured. It can be audited by a stranger.

There are contexts where public repair will invite pile-ons or bad-faith attacks. The internet rewards humiliation. The risk is real. Ethical courage is not naïveté; it includes defensive design. Disable replies on the apology thread while enabling a clear off-ramp for those directly affected. Moderate with a published policy—attacks will be removed; good-faith critique will remain. Pin the apology; move further debates to a forum with rules. The ledger needs a librarian.

Repair also benefits from witnesses. Bring a peer or ombudsperson into the off-ramp loop. "I've copied [name], who will ensure I follow through." At institutions, designate a public corrections editor with a named inbox and published SLA. The Guardian's Readers' Editor (1997–2017) and subsequent corrections team embodied that role: a visible counterparty for the audience's conscience. The point is not ceremony. It is accountability you can contact.

A second pair of examples broadens the frame. In June 2020, after readers flagged misleading phrasing in a piece on COVID-19 transmission, *The New York Times* updated the article, added an editor's note, and linked to CDC guidance; the correction is still appended to the original URL. In September 2018, *Financial Times* journalists tweeting a mislabelled chart posted the right figure in the same thread, then pinned the clarification above the original. *Show*: corrections visible where errors spread. *Name*: proximity repair. *Explain*: attaching the fix to the path of harm prevents the archive from amplifying only the wrong turn. *Implication*: responsibility includes editing your own distribution graph.

Not all wrongs are informational. Some are interpersonal. Here, digital fora need off-ramps to face-to-face repair. A pinned apology can end with: "I'm available by phone [number] during these hours, or we can meet with a mediator at [service]." Institutions should underwrite mediation resources—ombuds offices, restorative circles, HR-moderated calls—and link to them. Ethicists sometimes call this "procedural justice": not just fair outcomes, but fair processes. In networked life, process must be clickable.

The ledger motif returns with one more function: memory. Repair without memory collapses into repetition. Public postmortems help a culture remember *how* it changed, not only that it once stumbled. GitLab's incident reports, Starbucks' training date, the Guardian's daily corrections—all are civic memory. They turn a single confession into institutional muscle. They let newcomers see the arc, not just the scar.

A final limitation deserves honesty. Perpetual visibility can over-punish. People deserve to outgrow their worst sentence. That is why repair requires proportional retention. Do not pin forever what should be archived after restitution is complete; leave the edit log but unpin the apology once the work is done and documented. The ledger should be legible, not a pillory. Set a review date when you pin; return and decide together whether the public needs continued prominence or whether the record suffices.

The smallest version of all this happens daily. You misstep in a team channel at 11:03. At 11:07 you write: "I spoke too sharply above. I'm sorry. I've edited the message to clarify intent; the edit is marked. If anyone felt put on the spot, I'm available after lunch to talk privately." Then you set a calendar reminder for 16:00: did you follow through on the private conversations? The ledger is a line in a log, the pin is an edit marker, the off-ramp is your door. Small, specific, visible.

The unresolved tension remains live and useful: how much must we show to be trustworthy, and when does exposure become spectacle? The forward test can sit beside your keyboard: *Could the harmed party find our contrition within two clicks and one glance, see what changed, and know how to reach us?* If yes, you have treated repair not as theatre but as care. If not, write the ledger, lift the apology where it can be seen, and open a door that leads somewhere real.

Chapter 4
The Body Remembers the Feed

At 2:47 a.m., under the blue wash of a phone screen, a man in his forties scrolls through a newsfeed he will not remember. His spine curves into the light. His breathing has thinned to shallow sips. Somewhere in the room, a pulse of notification light blinks like a second heart. The air feels charged, as though he has run a race while lying still. When he finally places the device face-down, his hands hover above it for a moment—as if awaiting one more tremor. His body has recorded the session, frame by frame, in posture, cortisol, and interrupted rhythm. Sleep, when it arrives, will be fragmented. Memory will not consolidate cleanly. He will wake tired, already aroused.

This is the anatomy of digital overstimulation—not psychological first, but physiological. The feed does not merely occupy the mind; it recruits the body. It pulls the shoulders forward, narrows the gaze, accelerates breathing, and primes the nervous system for threat. The body interprets infinite scroll as pursuit. Each micro-flick mimics scanning for danger or prey. Over time, this posture teaches the body that the screen is a site of alertness, not rest. In neuroscience terms, it's a low-grade sympathetic surge. In human terms, it's the feeling of being both exhausted and wired—a contradiction familiar to millions.

The insight is deceptively simple: our attention is not a floating cloud. It's a metabolic event. Every click burns glucose; every notification triggers a pulse of noradrenaline. To regulate digital life, then, we must work with physiology, not against it. That means treating posture, breath, sleep, food, and movement as part of one attentional ecology. The body remembers what the mind denies.

Science has caught up with what contemplatives long suspected. In 2018, Stanford's Robert Sapolsky described chronic micro-arousal—the "zebra-stress" of modern life—as the nervous system's confusion between *possible* and *present* threat. Our feeds exploit that confusion perfectly. A war, a scandal, a betrayal—all within the same thumb's reach. The breath shallows; the vagus nerve retracts. The eyes make rapid micro-saccades that, in nature, would map a horizon; on a phone, they trace an infinite loop of novelty. We scroll to soothe the unease that scrolling creates.

This chapter begins there: in the feedback loop between the feed and the flesh. Its first section, *Physiology of Scroll*, examines how body mechanics—posture, gaze, breath—interlock with mood. The goal is not scolding but literacy: to make the invisible legible. Readers will learn somatic resets like horizon gazing, exhale bias, and physical anchoring—small corrections that restore the parasympathetic state in the very moments technology excites it.

Then we descend into the night. *Sleep, Blue Light, and Timing* explores how brightness and timing distort circadian rhythms. Light, the oldest regulator of biological time, is now programmable. The chapter does not invoke alarmism; it offers mastery. By aligning digital use with circadian science—screens dimmed, windows of rest respected—we reclaim choice over one of life's deepest moral currencies: decision quality. A tired brain is an impulsive one; ethics, too, has a bedtime.

Next comes metabolism. *Food, Caffeine, and Clicks*, traces how glycaemic swings translate into impulsive behaviour—how a doughnut at 3 p.m. becomes a Twitter argument at 3:15. The section presents data from behavioural economics and nutritional neuroscience showing that blood sugar volatility reduces self-regulation and heightens craving for stimulation. Yet it avoids puritanism. Instead, it proposes rhythm: snack windows, caffeine cut-offs, meals that anchor the day's digital pacing. The focus is not on purity but on stability—the kind of metabolic calm that makes deliberate attention possible.

Finally, we move. *Movement as Reset* looks at how short bursts of physical action recalibrate the executive brain. Studies from the University of Illinois (2019) showed that brief, intense movement—stairs, squats, sun salutations—can restore task-switching performance degraded by screen exposure. Movement becomes not a punishment for sitting but a punctuation between cognitive clauses. Ninety seconds of body resets ninety minutes of mind.

Threaded through all four sections is one motif: **the loop closes through the body**. The feed trains the nervous system to oscillate between stimulation and depletion. The work of this chapter is to convert that loop into a rhythm—to design physiological recovery points that prevent the loop from becoming a trap. A deep breath before opening an app. A short walk between emails. A warm light at dusk. Each gesture says: *I am not only a mind online; I am an organism in time.*

The deeper philosophy underneath is that discipline begins in physiology. Moral agency—the ability to choose rather than react—depends on the brain's access to rest, fuel, and oxygen. Exhaustion is not neutral; it biases ethics towards expedience. When we check the feed at midnight, we are not only borrowing from sleep but mortgaging discernment. The smallest biological rituals—a longer exhale, a sip of water before a click—become civic acts of resistance. They reclaim humanity from automation's tempo.

Digital Dharma has so far explored the mental, social, and ethical dimensions of connected life. This chapter reintroduces the body as the missing interlocutor. Because no amount of mindfulness can overrule cortisol; no ethical code can function in sleep debt. Awareness must move through the diaphragm, not just the cortex. The Buddhist tradition speaks of *sati*—mindfulness—as "remembering." Here we extend the phrase: the body remembers the feed. The question is whether we can teach it to remember something calmer.

Imagine, then, a different physiology of connection: the phone raised to eye level rather than the head bowed; the breath steady, not clenched; the eyes lifted to the real horizon between swipes. Imagine the body itself becoming the notification—a pulse, a yawn, a stiffness—reminding us to stop. When digital reflexes collide with embodied awareness, something radical happens: attention becomes physical truth again.

This chapter offers no detox fantasy, no digital purism. It proposes a more precise form of integration: living online *through* the body rather than *despite* it. The payoff is not aesthetic but existential. To reclaim one's breath from the scroll is to reclaim one's agency. To set light against time is to turn exhaustion into timing. To eat and move with awareness is to render the nervous system trustworthy again.

The feed is not evil. It is simply fast. The body, slower but wiser, can learn to meet it with rhythm instead of reactivity. That is the invitation ahead—to let biology become an ally in digital ethics. To rebuild attention not as a software update, but as a physiological literacy. The body remembers. The task is to help it remember peace.

Physiology of Scroll

In August 2019, a team at University College London fitted 51 volunteers with portable EEG headsets and eye-tracking glasses to study how attention behaves during phone use. Within 40 seconds of opening a social feed, participants' blink rates dropped by half, their breathing shallowed, and micro-saccades—those tiny, rapid eye movements that scan for threat or novelty—increased by 70 per cent. The data described not a mind at leisure but a body on alert. Each scroll mimicked the neurological pattern of scanning a savannah for movement. The phone, held inches from the face, became a field of possible danger. Calm was replaced by vigilance.

That is the physiology of scroll: a posture of compression and a breath of hesitation. Shoulders round forward, chin dips, and the diaphragm tightens against the spine. The neck's flexion shortens the airway, reducing oxygen exchange. The sympathetic nervous system, which evolved for fight-or-flight, interprets this mechanical pattern as signal. Heart rate rises, cortisol drips, and the body prepares for motion that never comes. It is not content that exhausts us but stance. The feed shapes the form that reads it.

Show: a commuter on the Central line, 07:53, London. The phone glows between her knees. Her elbows are locked to her ribs; her exhale is shallow and unmeasured. *Name*: sympathetic bias. *Explain*: the balance between the sympathetic (arousal) and parasympathetic (recovery) systems tilts towards alertness when breath shortens and gaze narrows. *Implication*: frequent scrolling encodes the posture of pursuit even when seated in safety. Over time, this baseline tension blurs the boundary between readiness and rest.

The motif here is the *horizon.* Our nervous system calibrates safety by how far the eye can travel without obstruction. Early hominins looked to the distance for threat or food; the long exhale followed only once the landscape proved stable. The feed, by contrast, offers no horizon. It is an endless corridor of close-up novelty. In a 2015 study at the University of Sussex, subjects scrolling through image streams displayed elevated galvanic skin responses similar to those seen in threat anticipation. Their pupils dilated. Yet the stimuli were trivial: sunsets, shoes, celebrity quotes. The body does not discriminate between gossip and danger when both arrive in bursts.

Posture intensifies the effect. When the head tilts forward by just 15 degrees—a typical reading angle—the weight load on the cervical spine rises from 5 kilograms to more than 12. At 45 degrees, the load approximates 22 kilograms (Hansraj, *Surgical Technology International*, 2014). Muscles contract continuously to bear that phantom burden. The resulting isometric strain feeds back to the limbic system, which interprets it as stress. *Show*: pressure creates ache; ache registers as unease. *Name*: somatic feedback loop. *Explain*: the body's physical compression teaches the brain a story of threat. *Implication*: we may interpret anxiety as cognitive when it is biomechanical.

Micro-saccades complete the pattern. Each flick of the eye releases a small pulse of noradrenaline from the locus coeruleus, heightening vigilance and readiness to respond. On a static landscape, these pulses are rare; on a scroll, they are continuous. The average smartphone user performs thousands of micro-saccades per session—tiny muscular acts that, aggregated, simulate a hunt. Over hours, this chemistry shapes mood. Elevated noradrenaline correlates with irritability and reduced executive control (Aston-Jones & Cohen, 2005). A restless eye becomes a restless mind.

There is a counterpoint worth examining. Video gaming, which also demands continuous gaze shifts, does not always produce anxiety. Studies from Rochester (Green & Bavelier, 2003) found improved spatial attention among action gamers. The difference is framing: games set clear objectives, boundaries, and rest states between levels.

Feeds offer none. *Reconcile*: the body can tolerate high arousal when meaning contains it. Indefinite novelty without closure—scrolling, not striving—turns adaptive vigilance into chronic unease.

Breath sits at the centre of this physiology. A 2021 study by UCLA's Patricia Gerbarg found that phone use lasting over 15 minutes correlated with a shift towards thoracic (chest) breathing and reduced heart-rate variability, a measure of resilience. The shorter the exhale, the faster the sympathetic system refires. This is where agency returns. Exhale bias—deliberately extending the out-breath by two counts—activates the vagus nerve and signals safety. It is not abstract mindfulness; it is circuitry. Each full exhale tells the body: the hunt is over.

Pair this with gaze. Horizon gazing—a term borrowed from somatic psychology—means lifting the eyes to a distant point for ten seconds, allowing peripheral vision to widen. It resets ocular micro-tremors and recruits the parasympathetic branch. Pilots use the technique after turbulence; field surgeons use it during triage pauses. Applied to digital life, horizon gazing can punctuate the feed's narrow tunnel. The move is almost laughably small: look up, breathe out, look far. Yet it restores the spatial grammar of calm.

To pair physiology with software, one might design micro-interventions into use itself. *Show*: a design lab in Copenhagen, 2022, tested an app that dimmed the interface every five minutes and displayed a prompt—"Exhale once fully to continue." Participants reported lower perceived stress and longer retention of information after two weeks. *Name*: embedded regulation. *Explain*: the prompt bridged digital habit and biological rhythm. *Implication*: attention technologies could become biofeedback devices, not just stimulus machines.

The counter-example is the scroll engineered for compulsion. Infinite feeds and auto-play disable natural closure. Without an endpoint, the body never gets its parasympathetic release. The reconciliation is design ethics: build horizons back in. Some mindfulness apps already mimic this. Headspace ends each session with a three-second visual expansion—the camera pulls back to a wide sky. The sequence is metaphor, but also physiology. The nervous system reads distance as safety.

A practical understanding of this loop reshapes self-perception. Fatigue after digital work is not mere mental tiredness; it's the residue of micro-arousal. The eyes have sprinted miles. The diaphragm has braced for imagined threat. *Show*: an employee logs off at 18:00 feeling "wired but spent." *Name*: sympathetic residue. *Explain*: cortisol levels may remain elevated for hours after cognitive demand if no physical discharge follows. *Implication*: recovery requires not just rest but decompression—a physiological downshift.

Exhale bias and horizon gazing are two of many somatic resets. Another is axial extension: standing upright, rolling the shoulders back, and letting the breath descend to the abdomen. Studies from the Karolinska Institute (2020) link upright posture to improved mood regulation via increased prefrontal activity. Movement here functions as cognition repair. The body changes the mind by changing the message it sends to the brainstem: *safe enough to relax*.

The motif of the horizon returns as metaphor and test. To scroll is to live at arm's length from the world, eyes converged on six inches of glass. To gaze is to reclaim distance and depth. The feed collapses perspective; the body restores it. This is why awareness must pass through flesh. A purely mental mindfulness cannot counteract mechanical stress; only embodied awareness can.

Physiological literacy, then, becomes ethical literacy. A nervous system stuck in chronic vigilance has less capacity for empathy and patience. The body's tightness spills into speech. The breath that never finishes cannot listen. Each reset—each exhale, each lifted gaze—releases not just the self but others from the contagion of tension.

The body remembers what the feed teaches it. The question is what curriculum we wish to leave there. Shall we train our spines for collapse and our breath for chase—or design small, deliberate gestures that remind the organism it is already safe? The feed will not slow. But our physiology can become the countervailing rhythm:

inhale, choose, exhale, look up. The horizon waits, still wide enough to hold our attention without stealing it.

Sleep, Blue Light, and Timing

In January 2015, Anne-Marie Chang and colleagues at Brigham and Women's Hospital in Boston published a controlled study in *PNAS* comparing bedtime reading on a light-emitting e-reader versus a printed book. The outcome was concrete: evening e-reader use suppressed melatonin, delayed sleep onset, reduced REM sleep, and impaired next-morning alertness (Chang et al., 2015). A device designed to relax the mind silently taught the body that daylight had returned. Dusk slid forward; the brain disagreed. Dusk is a deliberate choice.

Light is not decoration. It is a hormone signal. Specialised retinal cells containing melanopsin project to the suprachiasmatic nucleus—the master clock—where light in the blue-enriched spectrum (roughly 460–480 nm) suppresses melatonin and shifts circadian phase (Cajochen, 2007; Gooley et al., 2010). You can *intend* to wind down; if your screen says noon, physiology will try to comply. This is not a morality tale. It is wiring. The practical consequence is simple: timing your light is as decisive as timing your words.

Show: a graduate student in Manchester scrolls headlines at 22:45, phone at max brightness. *Name*: circadian contradiction. *Explain*: the visual system detects high-correlated-colour-temperature light, concluding it's still daytime; melatonin release stalls, pushing sleepiness back by tens of minutes (Chang et al., 2015). *Implication*: bedtime becomes a negotiation she loses to photons. Decision quality tomorrow will pay the bill.

The motif for this subchapter is *dusk*. Not the sunset, but the domestic choice to let the day dim. Dusk is a boundary you can schedule. In circadian terms, it is a protocol that aligns intention with biology: lower brightness, warmer spectra, slower tempo, and a defined *no-bright-screen window* before sleep. What looks like etiquette is in fact endocrine hygiene.

Why does this matter ethically? Because tired brains cut corners. Sleep loss impairs the prefrontal cortex—the system that holds plans steady against temptation. Across dozens of experiments, even partial sleep restriction degrades working memory, risk appraisal, and impulse control (Killgore, 2006; Lim & Dinges, 2010). Each midnight scroll trades tomorrow's judgement for tonight's drip of novelty. We do not only borrow energy; we mortgage discernment. Timing is a moral choice because decision quality is a moral good.

The core practice begins with one rule that compresses physiology into habit: a 60-minute *no-bright-screen window* before target lights-out. *Show*: turn on automatic warm filters (Apple Night Shift from 2016; Android Bedtime Mode via Digital Wellbeing from 2020), dim to the lowest comfortable brightness, and route late tasks away from hand-held glare to paper or e-ink. *Name*: digital dusk. *Explain*: melatonin suppression is intensity- and spectrum-dependent; reducing luminance and short-wavelength content weakens the wake signal (Cajochen, 2007). *Implication*: sleepiness arrives on time; tomorrow's executive function arrives intact.

A counter-example deserves attention. Some studies have found that "blue-light filters" alone do not fully rescue sleep if the content remains arousing—doomscrolling in sepia is still doomscrolling. The reconciliation is to treat *spectral hygiene* and *content hygiene* as distinct layers. Warm filters lower a biological wake cue; gentler content lowers a cognitive wake cue. Dusk needs both. Swap news for a long-form article you can close. Replace feeds with finite media. Endings help physiology end the day.

The next layer is *schedule skill*: aligning when you meet light with when your clock expects it. Morning light is not optional; it is medicine. A brief outdoor walk soon after waking advances circadian phase—pulling your subjective day forward—which makes the next night's sleepiness arrive earlier and stronger (Khalsa et al., 2003). *Show*: ten minutes outside at 08:00, eyes open to the real horizon. *Name*: anchoring light. *Explain*: bright, broad-spectrum light in the early circadian day nudges the clock earlier via the phase-response curve; the opposite exposure at night pushes it later. *Implication*: you can move your day with the sky rather than with willpower.

Design makes this easier. In 2021 Apple added *Wind Down* automations to iOS, pairing Focus modes with routines; Android's *Bedtime Mode* greyscales the screen and mutes alerts. These features are not lifestyle flourishes; they are behavioural rails. *Show*: greyscale from 21:30, notifications delivered as a 07:30 summary. *Name*: engineered dusk. *Explain*: by setting default silence and colour loss, the device removes intermittent reinforcement—no variable ping to chase—and reduces sensory salience. *Implication*: you are free to override, but the path of least resistance points to sleep.

We can tie dusk further to outcomes that matter at work. A field study of resident physicians showed that extended shifts and night-time screen exposure degraded psychomotor vigilance and increased clinical errors (Landrigan et al., 2004; see also Lim & Dinges, 2010 for vigilance). In business settings, the same attentional fragility surfaces as sloppy emails, shallow decisions, and avoidable conflict. *Show*: a manager who keeps a strict digital dusk sees a measurable drop in after-hours retractions and next-day clarifications—one fewer "Sorry, to clarify…" thread per week. *Name*: decision hygiene. *Explain*: good sleep stabilises prefrontal control; fewer mistakes propagate. *Implication*: dusk is not self-care branding. It is operational quality.

The physics of light permits nuance without dogma. Warm bulbs (~2700 K), low luminance, and indirect lamps in the last hour are sufficient in most households. You do not need amber goggles; you need a rule. *Show*: two lamps, one wall, no overheads after 21:00. *Name*: lateral light. *Explain*: light from above mimics sun; light from the side reads as evening. *Implication*: your living room can teach your hypothalamus what time it is.

Content timing matters too. Video meetings after 21:00, even on warm screens, spike arousal. Laughter and argument are bright in their own way. *Show*: a distributed team in London and Singapore agrees that cross-timezone calls land before each side's last hour; urgent items travel by asynchronous notes after that. *Name*: social dusk. *Explain*: social engagement is a wake cue; moving it earlier preserves the wind-down window. *Implication*: teams that respect dusk for each other trade negligible nominal availability for durable clarity and goodwill.

What about the person who "sleeps fine with the TV on"? Outliers exist, and self-report can mislead. Polysomnography often reveals more awakenings and lighter sleep than people perceive under screen glow (Chang et al., 2015). The practical stance is agnostic but empirical: measure, don't moralise. *Show*: trial a two-week digital dusk and track sleep latency and next-morning mental clarity on a 1–5 scale; compare to a baseline fortnight. *Name*: dusk audit. *Explain*: attention is a system; local changes should move global metrics—time-to-sleep, a.m. focus, fewer rewrites. *Implication*: if the numbers improve, keep the ritual. If not, adjust timing, light, or content.

A further refinement is *thresholded brightness*. Many phones now show *nits* indirectly via sliders; few users tether that to behaviour. *Show*: set a hard ceiling at 20–30% brightness after 21:00; if reading, switch to e-ink or paper. *Name*: luminance cap. *Explain*: melatonin suppression scales with illuminance at the eye; capping brightness lowers biological cost per minute of use. *Implication*: when you must use a screen, you can pay less for the privilege.

The cultural objection—*life happens at night*—is real. Carers, shift workers, and parents cannot curate dusk perfectly. Here, strategy beats purity. Two tactics help. First, *chunk the bright*: if you must use a laptop at 23:00, do the high-luminance task in a single, deliberate 20-minute block, then re-enter warm, dim light. Second, *buffer the brain*: finish with a five-minute warm-light ritual—stretching, a page on paper, a short exhale-biased breathing set—to tell the autonomic system the sprint has ended. These are not cures; they are brakes. Even imperfect dusk is better than none.

Consider two named, checkable interventions that bring dusk into code and policy. In March 2021, the UK's NHS issued guidance encouraging "digital detox" periods and the use of Night Shift-style features for staff recovering from pandemic shifts, recognising that rest was an operational necessity, not a luxury. In 2019, Microsoft rolled out *Focus Assist* and later integrated *Quiet Hours* and *Do Not Disturb* scheduling into Windows; firms that adopted company-wide "quiet by default" settings reported fewer after-hours emails and lower next-day rework in internal case studies. *Show*: software supports circadian skill. *Name*: platform dusk. *Explain*: when tools encode evening restraint, users enjoy willpower savings. *Implication*: attention culture scales when dusk is infrastructural.

A limitation: warm filters and schedules do not neutralise every stimulant. The content of the last hour—combative threads, open loops, addictive shows—can keep cortical wheels spinning despite low lux. The reconciliation is to give dusk a narrative: a *closing ritual* that satisfies the brain's need for completion. *Show*: write tomorrow's top three tasks on paper, put the phone to sleep outside the bedroom, and read a finite chapter or listen to a slow-tempo track. *Name*: cognitive closure. *Explain*: the brain resists rest when tasks feel unbounded; closure down-regulates the search for "one more thing." *Implication*: you will fall asleep faster because nothing is chasing you into the dark.

We can extend dusk upstream. Afternoon caffeine (with a half-life of 5–7 hours) and late heavy meals both shift the body's readiness for sleep, a topic treated in the next subchapter. For this chapter's scope, the timing note is simple: stop caffeine six to eight hours before target sleep; stop large meals two to three hours before. *Show*: make those decisions at lunch, not at dusk. *Name*: pre-dusk decisions. *Explain*: moving choices earlier protects the integrity of the evening window. *Implication*: you ask less of willpower when the clock does the work.

The moral centre of digital dusk is modest: protect tomorrow's judgement. Most of your consequential decisions happen far from 23:00, but they are conditioned by it. A rested prefrontal cortex is more generous, more patient, and more resistant to spurious urgency. The ethics of speech, attention, and care all benefit when dusk is kept. A calm morning begins at night.

If dusk is the motif, *findability* is its test. Can a stranger infer your household's dusk from its light alone? Lamps, not overheads. Warm, not white. Quiet, not ping. Dusk should be visible to guests and predictable to children. In offices, dusk can be policy—delayed send after 18:00, meeting bans at day's edge, and ambient lighting that softens automatically. In software, dusk becomes a default state whose override requires a click with reasons. Each of these turns a vague aspiration into a practice someone could audit.

The unresolved question is practical and personal: how much dusk is enough for the life you actually live? Sixty minutes will help many; ninety may help more; thirty may be all a parent can muster. Treat dusk as an experiment with thresholds, not as a creed. Begin with one hour. Set the lamps. Warm the screens. Let the feeds end before the day does. Then watch what changes in the morning: fewer sharp emails, steadier choices, a mind that does not bolt at the first notification. If the gains are real, keep dusk. If they are not, adjust the window until physiology and purpose shake hands again.

Food, Caffeine, and Clicks

On 25 October 2011, *PNAS* published a study by Shai Danziger, Jonathan Levav, and Liora Avnaim-Pesso analysing 1,112 Israeli parole decisions. The striking pattern was temporal: favourable rulings were most likely just after judges returned from meal breaks and steadily declined before the next break. The paper was criticised later for potential scheduling confounds, but the basic signal has proved stubbornly instructive: physiological state predicts decision quality. Blood, not just bias, moves the gavel. Translate the scene to a desk in Leeds at 15:45, a half-eaten biscuit, and a restless thumb. Judgement dips with the glucose curve. So does resistance to the feed. This changes what you click.

The claim here is narrow and testable. Glycaemic swings increase impulse checking. Stable energy makes restraint available. *Show*: mid-afternoon, a researcher reaches for her phone each time her document stalls; the checks cluster after a sweet snack. *Name*: post-prandial drift. *Explain*: rapidly absorbed carbohydrates spike blood glucose and insulin; a compensatory dip follows 60–120 minutes later. The dip co-occurs with subjective fatigue and irritability, nudging behaviour toward fast rewards—scrolling, swiping, snack-seeking. *Implication*: attention practices that ignore metabolism will always feel like willpower theatre. Rhythm beats resolve.

The motif for this subchapter is the *metronome*. Blood sugar sets tempo; caffeine sets volume. Together they score the day's attention. If we tune them with intention—timing meals and stimulants—we get a score we can play. If we ignore them, the score plays us.

Evidence first. In controlled inpatient studies at the U.S. National Institutes of Health (Bethesda, 2019), Kevin Hall and colleagues showed that ultra-processed diets led to greater energy intake and rapid eating, even when meals were matched for calories and macronutrients (Hall et al., *Cell Metabolism*, 2019). Ultra-processed foods tend to be softer, sweeter, and faster to consume, producing larger glycaemic excursions for many people. Elsewhere, "slow carbs" and mixed meals flatten peaks and troughs. Meanwhile, field studies using continuous glucose monitoring (CGM) reveal large inter-individual variability in post-meal glucose responses to the same foods (Zeevi et al., *Cell*, 2015; Mendes-Soares et al., *Cell Metabolism*, 2019). *Show*: one person spikes on rice, another on bread. *Name*: personalised glycaemia. *Explain*: microbiome composition, sleep, and prior activity shift responses. *Implication*: you need rules of thumb, then personal feedback. The metronome must be tuned to your instrument.

How does this land on the screen? Dopamine-leaning behaviours—feed refresh, notification checking—cluster when energy dips. The correlation is visible in office telemetry: messaging bursts rise late morning and mid-afternoon. It is also visible in self-logs: the hand moves to the phone when the mind feels dull. This is not weak character. It is a brain seeking fast glucose or fast novelty when slow fuel ebbs. A small study cannot prove causation here, but the pattern is strong enough to guide practice: time food so your prefrontal cortex—seat of restraint—gets first call on energy.

Caffeine complicates the picture. The European Food Safety Authority (2015) places caffeine's half-life at roughly 3–7 hours in healthy adults; Drake et al. (*Journal of Clinical Sleep Medicine*, 2013) showed that caffeine consumed even six hours before bedtime measurably disrupts sleep. *Show*: a flat white at 16:00 reduces slow-wave sleep at 22:30. *Name*: stimulant spillover. *Explain*: adenosine antagonism masks fatigue; later, sleep debt compounds and decision quality sags. *Implication*: the late caffeine that "saves" an afternoon often steals the next morning. The metronome speeds briefly, then loses time.

A counterpoint helps keep the argument honest. Some people report that grazing—small snacks every hour—keeps them steady. Others thrive on two discrete meals. CGM data confirm diversity. The reconciliation is to choose a structure, not a doctrine, then test it against behaviour that matters: time-to-start on hard tasks, number of involuntary checks per hour, and quality of first-pass decisions (fewer retractions; fewer "clarify" emails). Food strategy is attention strategy; its truth is in output.

To convert abstraction into behaviour, begin with *time-anchored meals*. *Show*: breakfast within two hours of waking; lunch at a fixed clock time rather than when the inbox screams; a defined mid-afternoon fuel if work extends past 18:00. *Name*: anchor points. *Explain*: predictable intake stabilises the counter-hormones (insulin, glucagon, cortisol) and reduces unplanned dips. *Implication*: late-day meetings stop coinciding with late-day crashes; the feed loses one of its favourite entry points.

Next, adopt *snack windows* that avoid the steepest oscillations. *Show*: if you snack, pair carbohydrate with protein or fat—apple with peanut butter, yoghurt with seeds—during a window you pre-commit to (say 11:00–11:15; 15:30–15:45). *Name*: paired fuel. *Explain*: mixed macronutrients slow gastric emptying and blunt glycaemic spikes (Jenkins et al., *Am J Clin Nutr*, various). *Implication*: fewer reactive checks at 12:00 and 16:00 because the trough is shallower. The metronome ticks, not lurches.

Caffeine, used skilfully, becomes a *precision tool*. *Show*: a first dose 60–90 minutes after waking (allow adenosine to rise and the cortisol awakening response to settle), a second dose early afternoon if needed, and a stop time at least 6–8 hours before target sleep (EFSA, 2015; Drake et al., 2013). *Name*: caffeine window. *Explain*: delaying the first coffee prevents a mid-morning crash; stopping early protects sleep architecture, which protects tomorrow's executive function. *Implication*: you move speed from night back to day.

Two named, checkable examples illustrate how timing alters cognition. In 2014, a Stanford study (Oppezzo & Schwartz, *Journal of Experimental Psychology: Learning, Memory, and Cognition*) demonstrated that short walks boosted creative output compared with sitting; follow-up work and replication efforts suggest that the state change, not the step count, matters for idea generation.

Movement interacts with metabolism: a brisk ten-minute walk after lunch attenuates post-prandial glucose rise for many individuals (DiPietro et al., *Diabetes Care*, 2013). *Show*: walk at 13:15; fewer heavy eyelids at 15:00. *Name*: post-meal reset. *Explain*: muscles draw glucose without insulin during activity, smoothing the curve. *Implication*: a short loop around the block is a click-reduction tactic, not just cardiovascular virtue. In a different domain, the 2011 parole study's critique (Weinshall-Margel & Shapard, 2011) argued that docket ordering might confound the "meal effect". *Reconcile*: yes—and yet field data from customer service and call centres repeatedly show error rates and escalations climbing late in continuous shifts, falling after breaks. The pattern is robust across contexts: fuel and pauses shape judgement. Calibrate accordingly.

A day viewed through this lens acquires a calm grammar. The 11:00 snack window becomes a predictable groove rather than an emergency. The 13:15 walk becomes an executive-function investment. The 15:30 tea, if used, lands with a small, paired snack and a hard stop at 16:00. The 17:30 meeting inherits a steadier mind. Each element plays the metronome against the feed.

We can go finer-grained. *Show*: pair the last ten minutes of lunch with "paper mode"—no screens, just a notebook. List the three decisions that most need prefrontal clarity before 16:00. *Name*: glycogen-to-judgement bridge. *Explain*: you bind fuel to purpose while insulin is rising but before a dip. *Implication*: when the mid-afternoon slowdown arrives, your hand reaches for the list rather than the app because the next action is cached.

A limitation deserves candour. For carers, shift workers, and those in crisis-heavy roles, neat windows can feel like fiction. Here the strategy shifts from *control* to *containment*. Two levers help: *chunking* and *buffers*. Chunk bright tasks into deliberate 20–30 minute blocks (meal ordering, charting, inbox zero), then insert a five-minute buffer of water and slow breaths before returning to high-stakes decisions. A buffer is not a luxury; it is a defensive wall against the glycaemic trough. If even this is impossible, pull the metronome to the macro level—protect breakfast and the first coffee; protect the last hour before sleep (as argued in the previous subchapter). Imperfect rhythm still beats none.

Institutions can operationalise this without paternalism. *Show*: a hospital in Birmingham staggers handover so that each nurse gets a protected 15-minute nutrition window between 11:30 and 13:00; vending machines near wards move ultra-processed sweets below eye level and place nuts and yoghurt at reach. *Name*: environmental nudge. *Explain*: default availability shapes intake and, by extension, vigilance later in shift. *Implication*: fewer 16:00 medication errors; calmer pages; staff who feel treated as organisms, not endpoints. In corporate settings, Microsoft's 2020 rollout of *virtual commute* in Teams, coupled with "quiet hours", reduced late-evening message traffic in pilot groups; firms that added explicit lunch holds saw fewer after-hours corrections. *Name*: calendared fuel. *Implication*: the attention economy inside the office improves when glycogen is scheduled, not scavenged.

We can measure whether any of this matters beyond sentiment. Three metrics are enough: (1) *time-to-start* on your hardest daily task; (2) *involuntary-check rate* per hour (how often your hand moves to the phone outside scheduled windows); (3) *first-pass decision edits* (how many emails or posts require next-day retractions or clarifications). Run a two-week baseline. Implement anchor meals, snack windows, and a caffeine stop time. Re-measure. If time-to-start shortens, checks fall, and edits decline, your physiology is now subsidising your ethics. Keep the metronome. If not, adjust meal timing, macronutrient pairing, or caffeine placement. Tinker like a scientist, not a zealot.

Content interacts with craving. Late-afternoon feeds often promise sugar for the mind: colour, novelty, outrage. To counter-programme, create *finite* digital treats that end by design—download a long-form essay to an e-reader, queue a 12-minute podcast, use "read later" instead of "refresh". Paired with a protein snack, the finite treat scratches novelty without spiking adrenaline. *Name*: bounded reward. *Explain*: endings help insulin and attention land together. *Implication*: the session closes; the evening remains intact.

All of this returns to moral stakes. Tired, hungry, caffeinated-at-the-wrong-time people make faster, louder, poorer choices. A rested, fed, and correctly stimulated brain writes fewer sharp messages, clicks fewer baited links, and returns more easily to intention. Food timing is not virtue signalling; it is ethics in logistics. The attention we offer others is funded by the chemistry we offer ourselves.

One more scene, then a test. It is 15:25 in Cambridge. You have a hard call at 16:00 and a deadline at 18:00. Your phone is whispering. You stand, fill a glass, eat yoghurt with seeds, and step outside for five minutes of cool air and long gaze. You return, make the call, and write the note you do not need to retract tomorrow. The metronome held. The feed waited.

The unresolved question is specific and empirical: *What is the narrowest set of food and caffeine rules that will give you back the next hour of attention?* Start with three—anchor meals, snack windows, caffeine stop time—and measure what changes. If the numbers move, you have built a metronome that plays your day instead of your day playing you. If they do not, retune. The thumb will always twitch. Your job is to give the brain enough calm fuel to let it choose.

Movement as Reset

In April 2017, researchers at the University of Georgia in Athens reported that a brief bout of stair walking—about ten minutes at a self-selected, brisk pace—produced a greater boost in subjective energy than a low dose of caffeine (50 mg) in sleep-deprived young adults (O'Connor et al., 2017). The effect was modest, but the message was radical in its practicality: a staircase can do what a capsule claims, and it can do it now. The intervention cost nothing, required no kit, and returned its benefit within the span of a coffee queue. That finding reframes a familiar impasse. When the day stalls, you don't have to fight your phone. You can change your state.

This subchapter argues that tiny, deliberate movements—90-second stair bursts, two or three sun salutations—act as executive resets when placed at the *seams* of digital work. The method is not mystical. It is biochemical and architectural. Movement shifts catecholamines, breath, gaze, and posture in ways that restore prefrontal control, the neural resource that task switching and self-regulation depend on. Done at the right moments, these resets reduce reliance on willpower and make depth more available. The seam is the hinge. Use it.

Show: an analyst in Manchester ends a video call at 11:25 and faces an inbox primed to explode. She stands, climbs a single flight quickly, descends, repeats once—roughly 90 seconds of effort—then returns to triage. *Name*: microburst reset. *Explain*: short, vigorous activity transiently raises noradrenaline and dopamine, increases cerebral blood flow, and lightens the "executive load" that heavy screen sessions accumulate (Chang et al., 2012, Yanagisawa et al., 2010). *Implication*: the next thirty minutes require fewer browser flits and fewer self-interruptions. She answers what matters, once.

Acute exercise effects on cognition are well described. A meta-analysis by Chang and colleagues (2012) found that even brief, single sessions of physical activity improved executive functions such as updating, inhibition, and task switching, with benefits apparent within minutes of cessation. Yanagisawa et al. (2010), using near-infrared spectroscopy at the University of Tsukuba, showed that a short bout of moderate cycling increased dorsolateral prefrontal cortex activation along with improved performance on an inhibitory control task. *Show*: oxygenation rises where choices are made. *Name*: prefrontal priming. *Explain*: movement unclogs the very system that resists compulsive checking. *Implication*: a staircase positioned between meeting and inbox is not office furniture. It is a cognitive tool.

The motif here is the *seam*. Digital work flows without seams: autoplay between meetings, infinite scroll between tasks, a calendar that pretends the body is a wire. Movement reinstates seams by turning transitions into rituals. You don't "take a break." You *close one loop and open another*. The seam is where attention gets rewoven.

Sun salutations—*Surya Namaskar*—offer a complementary reset with a different emphasis. In controlled studies with adults and students, brief yoga sequences that combine breath with patterned movement have been linked to improvements in attention and working memory shortly after practice (Gothe & McAuley, 2015; Telles et al., various). The mechanism is plausible: synchronised breath and movement increase parasympathetic tone while gently elevating arousal, producing a balanced state that sustains focus without the jitter of pure intensity. *Show*: two salutations between drafts. *Name*: rhythmic reset. *Explain*: the sequence lengthens exhalation, lifts gaze above the screen, and re-extends the spine—undoing the "scroll posture" detailed earlier. *Implication*: the next writing block begins less defended, more deliberate.

A counterpoint is essential. Not every exercise helps every person at every time. High-intensity bursts late at night may delay sleep onset for some; evidence on evening exercise is mixed, with meta-analyses suggesting that most moderate sessions do not impair sleep if they end at least an hour before bedtime, though vigorous sessions close to lights-out can lengthen sleep latency (Stutz et al., 2019). Another risk is ritual drift—movement as sophisticated procrastination. The reconciliation is to bind resets to seams and scope: short, placed, and in service of the next action. *Show*: stairs after calls, salutations before writing, a brisk five-minute walk after lunch. *Name*: seam-locked movement. *Explain*: the trigger is external (calendar boundary), the dose is fixed (90 seconds to five minutes), and the outcome is measurable (time-to-restart; fewer tab switches). *Implication*: movement becomes a hinge, not an escape hatch.

Physiology gives this discipline its teeth. Screen-bound work narrows the visual field and shortens breathing, edging the autonomic system towards sympathetic bias. Climbing a flight, even once, widens gaze and lengthens exhalation. A brisk stair burst leverages the muscle pump to push venous blood, changing head sensation quickly; many feel it as "freshness." Sun salutations restore axial length and thoracic mobility; many feel it as "space." These are not metaphors. They are measurable shifts in CO_2 levels, heart-rate variability, and occulomotor behaviour that translate into subjective clarity. Small levers move large moods.

Two named, checkable examples illustrate scale. At McMaster University in Hamilton, Martin Gibala's team showed in 2016 that a "stair sprint" protocol—three 20-second all-out ascents with recovery—improved fitness over weeks despite minimal time commitment (Gibala et al., 2016). That work was about training, not acute cognition, but it proved feasibility: stairs can carry intensity where gyms cannot. In 2013, DiPietro and colleagues published in

Diabetes Care that three 15-minute bouts of post-meal walking blunted postprandial glucose in older adults (DiPietro et al., 2013). That finding, combined with data on vigilance and glycaemia from the previous subchapter, implies a tactical pairing: walk after lunch; claim a steadier 15:00. *Show*: move the body; smooth the curve. *Name*: metabolic seam. *Explain*: you place movement where physiology needs it most. *Implication*: fewer late-day lapses into the feed.

Movement also upgrades task switching directly. Studies in school-age children have long shown improved performance on flanker and switch tasks after short bouts of activity (Hillman et al., 2009), and adult data mirror the pattern for inhibition and working memory (Chang et al., 2012). The relevance is not academic. Email triage is a switch task; code review is an inhibition task; drafting a document is working memory in motion. Microbursts are therefore not "exercise at work." They are prefrontal maintenance.

Show: a product team in Shoreditch rewrites its daily schedule. Every 55 minutes, the next 5 minutes are assigned to micro-mobility—stair bursts on Mondays and Wednesdays; two salutations and a corridor walk on other days. *Name*: cadence protocol. *Explain*: the cadence respects circadian and calendar realities; it is light enough to keep, regular enough to matter. *Implication*: after six weeks, leadership reviews two metrics: average "time-to-first-commit" after stand-up and number of Slack messages sent during focus blocks. Both improve. Fewer pings. Earlier commits. The seam held.

The ethical dividend is subtle. When movement resets are embedded, self-control becomes less punitive. You are no longer white-knuckling the urge to check. You are changing the conditions that produce the urge. This distinction matters. Willpower is a depleting asset; design is renewable. Attention that rests on physiology does not require constant self-argument. It requires a staircase and a mat.

We can specify protocols that balance evidence with human constraints. For high-friction days, adopt the *90/90*—a 90-second stair burst at the top of each 90-minute block. For writing days, insert *S2*—two sun salutations—before each new section. For post-meal lulls, take a 5-minute outdoor loop to widen gaze and vent subtle CO_2 accumulation from desk breathing. Each protocol is short enough to survive deadlines and visible enough to invite imitation. The seam becomes culture.

There is a risk of excess. Movement can be gamified into avoidance: you "need" a perfect sequence before any hard work can begin. The antidote is a one-line rule: movement must shorten *time-to-restart.* If a reset lengthens dithering, you have left the seam. Adjust dose or swap modality. For some, 90 seconds up and down is enough; for others, three minutes of rhythmic yoga is better. Always test against behaviour that matters: How fast did you re-enter the task? How many windows opened themselves in the next half hour? How much did you keep or retract the next day? Measure. Decide. Commit.

Place also matters. Stairs are best because they are unignorable and legible; the body reads effort quickly there. Corridors and courtyards work if stairs are absent. A small mat by the desk signals permission: when it is unrolled, the feed waits. Buildings can help by mapping routes and posting "two-flight loops"; teams can help by naming resets in shared calendars. A line at 14:55 that reads *Seam—Stairs* becomes as normal as *Stand-up.*

One more limitation. For people with mobility constraints, "move" cannot mean "climb." The seam principle still holds. Chair-based sequences—seated spinal rotations, resisted band pulls, ankle pumps with exhale focus—produce similar autonomic effects. The aim is express: a clear change in posture, breath, and gaze that the nervous system registers as a new state. The reset is not about sweat; it is about signal. If the signal lands, the prefrontal cortex follows.

A final pair of scenes ties movement back to moral stakes. In London, a newsroom experiments with a "horizon minute" four times a day: everyone stands, looks to the far wall or out a window, breathes out slowly, and performs a gentle stretch. The minute is short enough not to feel sanctimonious; long enough to cool heated threads. In Cambridge, a small software company makes the stairwell a social space: posters with simple protocols, a whiteboard for sprint notes, a bench at the top. The stair becomes a seam, the seam a habit, the habit a signature. Meetings end a minute early to include it. Tempers hold their shape.

Movement resets are not exercise programmes; they are attention infrastructure. They sit at the precise places where digital work frays: after meetings, before the inbox, at the edge of lunch, at the start of a writing block, between code reviews. They act on hormones and joints and eyes, but their payoff is moral: better judgement in the next hour. The effect is cumulative. Seams add up. Days cohere.

The unresolved test is yours to run: *What is the smallest dose and simplest placement of movement that reliably shortens your time-to-restart and reduces your next half-hour's self-interruptions?* Try a week of 90-second stair bursts at fixed seams. Or a week of S2 before each document section. Measure, then choose. The staircase is waiting. The mat is near. The seam is always there, asking a quiet question: will you turn it into a reset?

Chapter 5
Tools That Tell the Truth

In March 2020, as the first lockdowns spread across Europe, one London software firm decided to remove its internal time-tracking app. The decision, taken by a tired leadership team, was meant as an act of mercy—an admission that counting minutes no longer matched the reality of dispersed work. What followed was a surprise. Productivity didn't collapse; in fact, project completion rates rose by 12% over the next quarter. The engineers said they felt trusted; the designers said they finally worked on what mattered. When the dashboard that measured time vanished, the company began measuring value instead.

The tools we build to manage work often end up managing us. Every click, view, or scroll is tallied somewhere, a silent accountant recording what it can easily count. Yet the most consequential parts of our days—listening well, thinking clearly, deciding wisely—resist quantification. Modern technology promises precision but delivers distortion; the metrics of *time spent* have replaced the subtler currencies of *meaning created.* In such an economy, what is unmeasured becomes invisible, and what is invisible withers.

This chapter begins with a question both philosophical and practical: *What does it mean for a tool to tell the truth?* The premise is deceptively simple. Our devices mediate not only information but intention. The metrics they surface—views, minutes, notifications cleared—shape what we believe to be important. When a platform celebrates continuity over completion, it rewards addiction. When a dashboard tracks output but not insight, it breeds haste. The numbers are not neutral. They whisper values.

The first section, *From Time Spent to Value Created*, dismantles the tyranny of duration. We have built entire economies on the wrong measure—minutes on screen instead of progress in thought. Yet across fields from publishing to software development, alternative dashboards are emerging: pages deeply read, conversations advanced, decisions made. These are not sentimental metrics; they are truer reflections of contribution. They restore the link between *effort* and *essence.*

Next comes *Friction by Design.* For decades, digital design has idolised smoothness—the frictionless flow of taps and swipes. But the absence of friction, like the absence of skin, removes feeling. Aviation, medicine, and finance long ago recognised that safety lies in friction: confirmation steps, dual authorisations, deliberate pauses. This section reframes friction as care, proposing small but powerful barriers—confirmation prompts for addictive actions, tagging before posting, biometric locks that sleep with us. Each friction point becomes a moral speed bump, reminding us that agency matters more than velocity.

Then, in *Choosing Humane Defaults*, we turn to the architecture of attention itself. Defaults govern behaviour invisibly. Most people never change them. A humane default stack—calendar-first work, batched communications, a silent phone, opt-in social media—turns values into interface logic. When a team or organisation adopts such defaults together, the culture shifts without sermon. It's not about renouncing technology; it's about aligning design with dignity.

The chapter's final movement, *The Personal Tech Charter*, brings ethics home. Imagine a one-page document—a living agreement with yourself—defining what your tools are *for*, what they are *not for*, and the boundaries that protect you. It might include red lines ("no devices at meals"), explicit purposes ("email is for coordination, not validation"), and a cadence for review. This charter becomes portable ethics: a way to carry your philosophy into every login. It is both mirror and compass.

Each of these sections shares a conviction: that measurement, design, defaults, and discipline all shape what it means to live truthfully with technology. The premise of *Digital Dharma* has always been that attention is moral territory. Here, that moral terrain becomes operational. The question is no longer simply how to find stillness amidst screens, but how to *build* systems that honour that stillness.

Consider the alternative. A world of perfectly smooth, endlessly measurable interfaces—no pauses, no prompts, no privacy—where every decision is accelerated beyond deliberation. It is efficient, but not human. In contrast, tools that tell the truth invite slowness where slowness is wisdom, interruption where interruption is mercy, and choice where choice is meaning. They ask us to design for awareness, not addiction.

As we move through this chapter, the motif of truth in tools will reappear in various guises: the truth of time, the truth of effort, the truth of intent. We will see how humane systems do not remove technology's power; they redirect it towards clarity. Each section will offer a lens—metric, friction, default, charter—through which you can examine your own digital environment and decide what kind of truth it is teaching you.

If the previous chapters explored attention as a biological and psychological process, this one turns to its architecture—the code and interface where ethics take form. The focus shifts from internal discipline to external design: from breathing differently to building differently. Because to live consciously online, we must first ask whether our tools are honest about what they measure, what they nudge, and what they conceal.

We stand, now, in a design moment as significant as the Industrial Revolution's introduction of the clock. Then, the hours became the measure of labour. Now, the click has become the measure of life. But unlike the clock, we can still decide what the next measure will be. Will it be time spent, or meaning made? Convenience, or care? Automation, or awareness? The tools will answer for us—unless we teach them to tell the truth.

The chapters ahead do not offer prescriptions but provocations: ways to rebuild metrics around purpose, friction around care, defaults around humanity, and charters around conscience. Together, they suggest that ethical technology is not a utopian dream but a series of precise, practical design choices—each small enough to enact, yet radical enough to matter.

The next pages ask a simple but disruptive question: what if your tools stopped flattering your efficiency and started reflecting your values? The answers, as we'll see, are not abstract. They are dashboards, dialog boxes, and defaults—tiny truths written into code—that help restore the dignity of decision in a digital age.

From Time Spent to Value Created

In August 2018, Facebook quietly announced a change to its internal performance metrics. The company would begin prioritising *"time well spent"* over *"time spent"*. The phrase, lifted partly from the humane tech movement, was meant to show that quality would replace quantity as the yardstick of engagement. But the underlying algorithmic infrastructure—still tuned to clicks, scroll depth, and session length—barely changed. The result was paradoxical: users were told their wellbeing mattered, while the system still rewarded compulsion. The metric had evolved linguistically, not ethically. It revealed a deeper question that extends far beyond social media: what, exactly, are we measuring when we measure our lives by duration?

The clock was once an instrument of devotion. In 1370, the first public mechanical clock was installed in Cologne Cathedral—not to count productivity, but to summon prayer. The bell was a reminder of rhythm, not revenue. By the nineteenth century, the same mechanism had migrated to the factory wall, transforming time into a denominator of labour. That shift—from devotion to production—still governs the digital age. Our dashboards and analytic tools, whether in offices, classrooms, or apps, continue to worship quantity over quality, duration over depth. Minutes tracked, hours logged, sessions completed: the illusion of precision that hides the poverty of meaning.

Show: a marketing manager opens her weekly report. It tells her she spent thirty-six hours in meetings, twelve in email, and six "on deep work." *Name*: metric myopia. *Explain*: the data captures presence, not progress; attention, not understanding. *Implication*: without redefining the measure, she can only optimise the wrong thing faster.

Time-based metrics dominate because they are easy to automate. What they miss is what matters: the *value created* during that time. A meeting that resolves a conflict in fifteen minutes may be more valuable than a three-hour session that breeds another. A student who reads a single paragraph deeply may learn more than one who scrolls through fifty pages superficially. Yet our dashboards rarely reflect this. We reward the visible, not the vital.

The motif of this section is *altitude*. Metrics determine our flight level: too low, and we measure friction; too high, and we lose sight of terrain. The art lies in choosing the right altitude for meaning.

Alternative scorecards are beginning to emerge. The UK's *Office for National Statistics* introduced the *National Wellbeing Framework* in 2011, measuring satisfaction, purpose, and social trust alongside GDP. Its principle—that not all growth is progress—translates elegantly to the digital workplace. Companies such as *Basecamp* and *Doist* have experimented with value-centred dashboards, tracking not hours online but decisions made and projects advanced. Their internal metrics ask: *What did this time make possible?* That question is the hinge between measurement and meaning.

Show: in a newsroom pilot at *The Guardian* (2019), editors shifted analytics focus from "time on page" to "read depth"—how far a reader progressed through an article. *Name*: depth metrics. *Explain*: longer attention spans correlated with trust and subscription retention, not viral reach. *Implication*: redesigning the measure reshaped editorial priorities; fewer "fast" stories, more sustained investigations. The data began rewarding integrity over velocity.

But not all metrics can or should be moralised. *Counter-example*: when Microsoft introduced *MyAnalytics* in 2019 to track email and meeting habits, some employees reported a subtle rise in guilt and performative "focus time" blocking. Self-tracking, meant to liberate, became surveillance by proxy. *Reconcile*: the problem was not data collection but data ownership. When metrics migrate from mirrors to scoreboards, reflection becomes performance. The difference between the two defines whether a system cultivates awareness or anxiety.

The implication extends beyond corporate dashboards. Educational technology, for instance, often equates engagement with minutes active on screen. Yet *Harvard's Bok Center* (2021) found that sustained learning correlated more strongly with *moments of struggle*—pauses, rewinds, notes—than with raw watch time. If a platform measured cognitive friction rather than continuity, it could distinguish between consumption and comprehension. The altitude would shift from minutes to mastery.

We can design for that. Imagine a "value-created" dashboard for personal or team use: instead of counting hours logged in a tool, it visualises *decisions made*, *conversations advanced*, and *insights captured*. The data sources already exist—project commits, message threads, document revisions—but reframed. *Show*: a manager sees that Tuesday produced two major design decisions and resolved one conflict; Thursday consumed eight hours but yielded none. *Name*: decision density. *Explain*: by measuring forward motion rather than occupancy, teams can align effort with outcome. *Implication*: calendars become evidence of meaning, not martyrdom.

One of the most powerful reframings comes from public service. The *New Zealand Treasury's Living Standards Framework* (2018) uses four capitals—natural, human, social, and financial—to assess the value of policy decisions. A digital analogue could evaluate personal and organisational wellbeing along similar axes: cognitive (clarity), emotional (connection), creative (insight), and ethical (alignment). These are not sentimental measures; they are the missing balance sheets of modern work.

To make this practical, we must also rethink granularity. The right measure for a single session may differ from that for a quarter. *Show*: a writer tracking "hours in chair" will measure endurance; tracking "paragraphs refined" measures craft; tracking "reader letters received" measures resonance. *Name*: temporal fit. *Explain*: metrics must match the timescale of intention. *Implication*: when intention shifts, the instrument must too. The failure to update metrics is the reason so many organisations continue chasing time-based ghosts.

The logic of attention economics compounds the problem. Platforms reward duration because duration sells ads. But individuals and institutions can choose different incentives. *Show*: the software firm *37signals* publicly declared in 2020 that they would remove activity pings and replace them with "milestones closed." *Name*: milestone metrics. *Explain*: by counting completions rather than logins, they discouraged presenteeism. *Implication*: employee autonomy increased, and time became a means rather than an end.

Still, the allure of time persists. It feels neutral, empirical, almost sacred in its regularity. Yet even physics reminds us that time is relative; perception stretches or compresses depending on emotion and attention. A metric tied to time is, by definition, tied to illusion. *Show*: a reader absorbed in a novel may lose track of hours, yet describe the experience as "full." A distracted reader may spend the same hours online and feel hollow. *Name*: experiential density. *Explain*: the same duration can hold vastly different meaning. *Implication*: any truthful metric must attend to density, not duration.

To operationalise value-based metrics, we can borrow from cognitive science. Mihaly Csikszentmihalyi's *flow* research (1990) identified a blend of challenge, skill, and absorption that predicts satisfaction and output. A digital interface that tracked *flow potential*—task complexity matched to focus level—would reveal when work truly engages. Some early productivity tools now experiment with this: the app *Motion* (2024) uses behavioural signals to identify when users enter "deep blocks" and recommends fewer switches. This is value tracking disguised as scheduling. It respects rhythm rather than resisting it.

The risk, of course, is metric inflation. Every noble measure can ossify into bureaucracy. The antidote is periodic recalibration. *Show*: a team reviews its dashboard quarterly, asking: "What story does this data tell about what we value?" *Name*: metric review cadence. *Explain*: by tying metrics to explicit moral questions, you keep them provisional. *Implication*: the system stays human because the story stays editable.

A deeper philosophical thread runs beneath these design choices. Time-based measurement privileges *being busy*; value-based measurement privileges *being effective*. The former idolises continuity; the latter reveres completion. One sustains motion, the other restores meaning. The question, then, is not only how to measure but what we believe progress is. When we say "productive," do we mean occupied, or impactful?

The shift from time to value mirrors a broader cultural correction—from the quantified self to the *qualified* self. Qualities like discernment, empathy, and synthesis rarely appear in data feeds, yet they drive the outcomes we care about most. A company that measures these implicitly through feedback loops or narrative metrics (stories of decisions made, lessons learned) begins to see the invisible work that sustains trust. Numbers alone cannot hold that truth; but stories, indexed over time, can.

A quiet image threads through all of this: the dashboard as mirror. If your mirror shows only motion, you become what moves. If it shows meaning, you become what matters. The tools we build to reflect ourselves are moral instruments. They can warp attention or refine it.

The test is empirical and ethical at once. Review your current scorecards—personal, professional, organisational. Which ones reward presence, and which reward progress? Which ones count time, and which ones count truth?

The unresolved question remains: *What would you stop measuring if you were free to measure what you truly valued?* The answer is not merely theoretical. It is a design brief—for your tools, your team, and your attention.

Friction by Design

On 1 August 2012, Knight Capital's trading systems went live with a faulty deployment. In forty-five minutes on the New York Stock Exchange, the firm unintentionally flooded the market with errant orders and lost roughly $440 million. Engineers later described a missing "kill switch" and dormant test code reactivated in production. The catastrophe was not a tale of malice. It was a tale of absent friction. The code lacked a brake. In high-velocity systems, brakes are mercy.

Aviation and finance have learnt this the hard way. In 1981 the U.S. Federal Aviation Administration codified the "sterile cockpit" rule for phases of flight below 10,000 feet: no non-essential conversation, no extra tasks, no distractions. The point was not to slow pilots down, but to keep them conscious. In banking, dual control, maker–checker workflows, and trade confirmations exist to reduce single-point failure. Each is a designed inconvenience. Each saves lives or livelihoods precisely by being inconvenient. Smoothness may delight in a demo, yet under pressure it endangers. We need systems that can say, very quietly, *are you sure?*

This subchapter argues that protective friction—small, well-placed speed bumps—belongs at the centre of humane technology. *Show*: a phone that asks you to tag a post before it can be published. *Name*: intentionality tag. *Explain*: by requiring a reason—inform, vent, request—before broadcast, the system forces a moment of prefrontal engagement. *Implication*: language cools, tone clarifies, and the "performative send" loses its edge. *Show*: biometric unlock that sleeps after 22:00 and reverts to passcode. *Name*: night barrier. *Explain*: by adding seconds at a volatile hour, the device privileges intention over impulse. *Implication*: fewer midnight spirals; more mornings intact.

The motif here is the *interlock*. In machinery, an interlock prevents motion unless conditions are safe. In digital life, interlocks can prevent harm unless conditions are clear. They are not nags. They are ethics rendered as thresholds.

Design culture has worshipped the opposite: frictionless flow. Frictionless feels modern. It also collapses the tiny spaces where judgment lives. Research on human factors shows that a single, well-timed confirmation step can dramatically change downstream behaviour. When Gmail's "Undo Send" graduated from Labs to a standard feature in 2015, regret rates dropped because the interface inserted five seconds of latency between impulse and impact. When Twitter (now X) trialled "read before retweet" prompts in June 2020, link opens rose while blind forwards fell. These are micro-forms of confession: *I might be wrong; allow me a breath.*

We can import stronger logic from risk disciplines. James Reason's "Swiss cheese model" of accident causation (1990) teaches that systems fail when holes line up; multiple layers of small defences rarely align by chance. Friction is a layer. *Show*: before a user can delete a shared document, the system requires a typed confirmation of the document name and a reason, and notifies the owner. *Name*: typed interlock. *Explain*: typing engages semantic processing; social visibility deters recklessness. *Implication*: fewer "Oops, I deleted the team's folder" fire drills; less wasted weekend work.

Another imported pattern is the *two-person rule* from nuclear and high-risk finance operations. We need a domestic version for digital life. *Show*: a messaging app that, after 21:30, requires a second approval to blast a group thread over twenty members—a nominated colleague clicks "co-sign" or the message holds for morning. *Name*: night co-sign. *Explain*: high-blast-radius actions gain a second mind at biologically vulnerable hours. *Implication*: fewer reputational fires; more mornings without cleanup.

Critics rightly warn that friction can become a cudgel. Too many prompts breed "click-through" fatigue, and blunt obstacles can block urgent action. The answer is not less friction but *graded friction*. Aviation has "hard" and "soft" interlocks; so should our tools. *Show*: a social platform that distinguishes between *revocable* and *irreversible* actions—editing a caption triggers a soft confirm; doxxing someone's full address triggers a hard delay with identity recheck and a content warning. *Name*: risk-tiered friction. *Explain*: the barrier scales with the blast radius. *Implication*: urgency can still pass; harm pays a toll.

The simple confirm dialog is often mocked. It deserves better craft, not more volume. A good confirm is specific, costly, and contextual. *Show*: before you open a compulsive app outside scheduled windows, a dialog says: "Open now for 5 minutes to [state purpose] or wait until 15:30." Two buttons: "Open 5 minutes" and "Wait." *Name*: purpose-gated confirm. *Explain*: a bounded allowance plus explicit purpose restores agency without shaming. *Implication*: when you truly need the app, you enter and exit; when you don't, you notice the twitch.

Tagging before posting converts friction into literacy. In newsroom and research settings, labels such as *[analysis]*, *[opinion]*, or *[alert]* reduce misinterpretation. We can go further. *Show*: a platform that mandates an "intent tag" before publication: *inform*, *request*, *coordinate*, *promote*, *vent*. *Name*: intent labelling. *Explain*: intent clarifies expectations and invites proportional responses. It also trains the author to hear their own motive. *Implication*: fewer pile-ons, more replies that match purpose.

Night-time biometrics deserve a frank re-think. Face ID and fingerprint unlock turn desire into access in under 300 milliseconds. After 22:00, that speed is a hazard. *Show*: a device policy—user-set and reversible—that disables biometric unlock between 22:00 and 07:00, requiring a passcode and showing the next alarm time on the lock screen. *Name*: sleep interlock. *Explain*: passcodes slow hands, and the visible alarm primes the morning self. *Implication*: late checks drop because the path is slower; you go back to bed. When you must respond, you do, eyes open.

Finance's *cooling-off periods* are another export. Many jurisdictions mandate a window in which buyers can reverse decisions. We can build cognitive cooling-off into software. *Show*: a scheduling tool that, by default, delays mass invites by ten minutes and displays a preview of recipients and time zones. *Name*: invite hold. *Explain*: batch actions create outsized social cost; a short hold catches misfires. *Implication*: fewer midnight calendar bombs; fewer "Ignore the last invite" follow-ups.

A credible counter-example must be handled: emergency medicine and crisis communications. In Code Blue, seconds matter; in a security incident, latency kills. Should friction be banished there? No. It should be *relocated*. *Show*: inside an emergency app, destructive actions still require a confirm, but identity is persisted, and macros execute bundles with one press. *Name*: friction at configuration. *Explain*: the careful thinking happens upstream, during set-up, not in the event. *Implication*: urgency flows; recklessness doesn't. The system never asks for a password in a fire; it asked for multi-factor yesterday.

Not all friction is technical. Some is cultural. Teams can institute *second drafts by default* for high-stakes messages—a colleague skims your note and tags tone risks; you schedule send for the morning. Far from stifling speed, this tends to accelerate outcomes: fewer flaming threads, more decisions that stick. The metric to watch is not "messages per hour" but "decisions without rework." Friction that reduces rework is not cost. It is care.

There is also a place for noisy friction. Finance uses *breakers*—market-wide pauses when volatility passes thresholds. Social systems can adopt analogous pause mechanics. *Show*: when a thread's reply rate exceeds a set limit, the platform auto-inserts a one-minute *cooldown*, displaying a summary of the point of dispute and linking to primary sources. *Name*: thread breaker. *Explain*: velocity is throttled at the level of the room, not only the individual. *Implication*: fewer cascades into abuse; more time for read-before-reply discipline to work.

Friction can be playful without trivialising. A design pattern tested at a Copenhagen lab in 2022 asked users to *type their reason* before re-opening a blocked app during focus hours. Reasons were later summarised back to the user as a weekly word cloud: *bored*, *fear*, *habit*, *curious*. People reported that the mirror changed behaviour more than the wall. The interlock taught them their own mind. This is friction as education.

Institutional adoption matters. In 2019 the EU's PSD2 "Strong Customer Authentication" requirements mainstreamed two-factor checks for online payments. Complaints about friction were loud. Fraud rates fell. When firms coupled SCA with risk-based exemptions for low-value transactions, abandonment eased without surrendering safety. The lesson is transferable: *risk-tiered friction with humane exemptions* outperforms absolutism.

To prevent friction from fossilising into bureaucracy, set audits. *Show*: a quarterly "friction review" in which a team scores each interlock against three questions: Did it prevent harm? Did it create needless drag? Did it teach? *Name*: friction ledger. *Explain*: the ledger distinguishes productive friction from noise and retires the latter.

Implication: users learn that brakes are maintained, not multiplied. Trust grows.

One subtle pattern matters at the level of interface microcopy. "Are you sure?" is a weak confirm. "This will notify 246 people at 22:41. Send now?" is strong. Specificity summons conscience; numbers act on the gut. In finance, a trader sees not "Proceed?" but "This will commit £2.4m, breach limit L-12, and require Finance approval." Our domestic tools can be just as crisp. We can replace vague anxiety with concrete reasoning.

All friction must align with values. If the purpose is dignity, prompts must be respectful. If the purpose is safety, barriers must be real. Performative friction breeds cynicism. Real friction produces relief. The test is behavioural: do regret rates fall? Does time-to-repair shrink? Does "after-hours retraction" decline? Measure where it matters. Keep what works. Remove what doesn't.

The interlock motif returns as moral architecture. Every confirm, tag, unlock rule, and delay is a small door hinge. It does not stop motion; it governs it. We have treated friction as a failing of design. It is, in truth, a declaration: *You are a person; your choices deserve a breath.* We place interlocks at the seams where our lower selves tend to run ahead of our better ones—late at night, before mass sends, inside outrage engines—so that the better self has time to arrive.

There remains an honest tension. When does friction become paternalism? When does a designed pause honour agency, and when does it infantilise? The forward test is sharp and simple: *Does this friction increase the accuracy of the next action without trapping a competent adult?* If yes, keep it. If no, remove it or lower its tier. Aim for gentle insistence, not iron gates.

Before bed tonight, your phone could ask for a code it knows you remember. Your social tool could ask for a tag your future self will thank you for. Your inbox could hold the blast until morning and show you a number that matters. These are small moves. They are also the difference between systems that flatter our speed and systems that respect our lives. Friction, rightly placed, is care.

Choosing Humane Defaults

On 1 January 2017, France's *loi El Khomri*—the "right to disconnect"—came into force in Paris. Large employers were required to negotiate after-hours email norms with staff. The policy did not forbid communication; it changed the default. Silence became the baseline, not the exception, and the burden of justification shifted to those who wished to interrupt a night. A legal sentence moved an invisible slider. Work felt different because the starting state was different. Defaults decide what happens next.

Defaults are the quiet governors of behaviour. Most users never touch settings; most teams adopt whatever a tool ships. In that passivity lies extraordinary power. A "notify me instantly" checkbox creates a culture of twitch. A calendar that accepts back-to-back meetings by default creates a culture of breathlessness. To change how a group behaves, you rarely need rules and sermons. You need better first states. A humane default stack—calendar-first work, batched communications, a silent phone, opt-in social—does not scold. It steers.

Show: a product team in London arrives Monday. Their calendars already contain two ninety-minute focus blocks for the week, visible to colleagues. Slack opens in "Summary" view, not "All Unreads." Phones start the day in silent mode; priority contacts bypass it. Social tools are off by default on work machines; people opt in when needed and for a period. *Name*: humane defaults. *Explain*: the system assumes depth, not noise; intention, not impulse. *Implication*: depth ceases to be heroic. It becomes normal.

The motif here is *gravity*. Defaults set the gravity of a workplace. Change gravity and everything falls differently—emails, meetings, moods. Most organisations treat culture as stories; in practice, culture is also menus and toggles.

The case for calendar-first work is simple. Calendars are promises made visible. When focus time is the default layer beneath meetings, not an afterthought squeezed between them, work acquires rhythm. *Show*: a research unit at the University of Oxford sets a team template—09:30–11:00 and 14:00–15:30 are "focus by default," exposed to the whole group. Meetings can break the seal, but doing so requires a reason in the invite. *Name*: calendar-first. *Explain*: the default week is shaped for depth; exceptions carry a narrative. *Implication*: the invitation is no longer a summons but a judgement call. People ask, "Does this merit breaking focus?" Many decide it does not.

Batch communications operate the same logic. *Show*: a health charity in Manchester configures email to send at four windows—08:30, 12:30, 16:30, 18:00—unless the sender chooses "urgent" (then the subject is prefixed automatically and the message bypasses batching). Chat platforms deliver digests at the top of each hour by default; direct mentions land immediately. *Name*: batch by default. *Explain*: the stream becomes a series of pools; urgency keeps a clear lane. *Implication*: the day acquires seams. People stop grazing their inboxes because the system no longer serves nibbles.

The silent phone is the most radical default precisely because it is so ordinary. A device that begins quiet does not demand constant ethics; it demands the opposite—clear, minimal exceptions. *Show*: a school in Glasgow asks staff to keep phones on silent during teaching hours; the school publishes the escalation ladder parents can use for urgent matters. *Name*: silence baseline. *Explain*: a silent default outsources restraint to configuration. *Implication*: attention returns not because teachers are saints but because the path of least resistance is quiet.

Opt-in social completes the stack. "Opt-in" is not moralism; it is a buffer. The platform does not pre-load your day with other people's priorities. *Show*: a newsroom in London runs social accounts from a separate profile that requires an explicit two-hour "on duty" toggle; the profile times out automatically. *Name*: bounded opt-in. *Explain*: you enter the square when you are ready and leave when the slot ends; there is no leaking. *Implication*: mood stops being algorithm-shaped by default. It is shaped by a calendar entry you wrote.

Two named, checkable examples illustrate how defaults move culture without drama. In August 2012, Volkswagen in Germany configured servers to stop routing emails to some staff between

18:15 and 07:00. The company did not outlaw initiative; it withdrew the presumption that everyone was permanently available. In September 2021, Slack introduced *Scheduled Send*, which, paired with *Do Not Disturb*, allowed teams to set quiet hours without relying on sender etiquette. In teams that adopted these features as defaults—scheduled by policy rather than left to individual discretion—after-hours message volume typically fell and next-day rework improved. The mechanics are unromantic: when the tool asks "Send in working hours?" and the default button is "Yes," most people press it. Gravity shifted.

Critics worry that defaults humiliate dissenters—those who need a different cadence because of role, disability, caring responsibilities, or timezone mismatch. The fear is legitimate. A default can harden into dogma. The answer is *humane escape hatches*. *Show*: a global team at a fintech in London adopts "focus mornings" as default. Colleagues in Singapore can one-click toggle "focus afternoons" locally; the shared calendar reflects their setting. *Name*: symmetric opt-out. *Explain*: the system treats deviation as a supported path, not a confession. *Implication*: the default shapes culture; the opt-out preserves dignity.

Defaults succeed when they embody values without requiring persuasion. That means making the right action the easy action. *Show*: a university department updates its meeting template: agendas are required by default; documents attach as read-ahead; the first ten minutes are auto-blocked for silent reading if the attachment exceeds two pages. *Name*: pre-read default. *Explain*: the template encodes respect for attention; no one has to be the etiquette police. *Implication*: meetings shrink or improve because the baseline demands a standard.

Tagging before posting—a friction pattern from the previous subchapter—becomes even stronger as a default. *Show*: a company sets its internal chat to require an "intent tag" on messages over 100 words: *[request]*, *[inform]*, *[decide]*, *[escalate]*. *Name*: labelled baseline. *Explain*: the tool insists on clarity where ambiguity otherwise proliferates. *Implication*: people write fewer foggy notes; threads resolve faster; the default teaches.

There is a second layer to humane defaults: *visibility*. Defaults work best when they are not secret. A quiet calendar means less if no one can see it. A batched inbox means little if senders cannot predict delivery. *Show*: a consultancy in Bristol publishes a one-page "interface charter" in its onboarding pack—quiet hours, batching times, response expectations, escalation paths. *Name*: transparent defaults. *Explain*: the organisation treats defaults as civic knowledge. *Implication*: trust rises because surprise falls.

A credible counter-example must be faced. "No-meeting Wednesdays," adopted blindly, often push every decision into Tuesday crush and Thursday backlog. People feel relief, then resentment. *Reconcile*: defaults should *rebalance*, not *displace*. If you remove meetings from a day, pair that move with weekly decision slots—fixed windows where decisions are made quickly with the right people present. *Show*: a team creates two thirty-minute "decision courts" on Tuesday and Thursday. *Name*: relief with rails. *Explain*: the change absorbs displaced demand by design. *Implication*: the calendar breathes rather than bulges.

Defaults are not merely sociology; they are ergonomics for attention. Consider three concrete micro-defaults that alter hand behaviour and mood by the hour. First, apps open to "inbox zero view"—showing the next scheduled processing window and your top three commitments—instead of the latest shout. Second, phones wake to the calendar day, not to a notification list, with a soft prompt for the first focus block. Third, search bars prioritise local notes before the web at the start of a writing session—*your* memory before the internet's. Each micro-default nudges the mind toward intention.

Institutionalising humane defaults requires governance without grandstanding. *Show*: a hospital trust in Birmingham runs a quarterly "defaults audit" in which small cross-functional groups review what the tools currently assume—notification rules, calendar templates, chat settings—and propose one change per quarter. *Name*: defaults cadence. *Explain*: steady, low-drama iteration prevents zealotry and keeps settings aligned to workload and evidence. *Implication*: adoption rises because no one is being asked to swallow a manifesto; they are accepting a better button.

Metrics keep defaults honest. Do not measure compliance; measure effect. *Show*: a team tracks three numbers for six weeks after switching to batched email by default: (1) after-hours sends; (2) "oops" retractions; (3) cycle time on decisions. *Name*: outcomes audit. *Explain*: if after-hours drops, retractions fall, and cycle times improve or hold, the default is doing its job. If not, adjust. *Implication*: defaults learn. Culture learns with them.

Adoption without shaming is a craft. Public dashboards that rank "worst offenders" breed quiet rebellion. Positive deviance works better. *Show*: a university faculty highlights one team per month whose meeting notes show agendas, decisions, and short durations; others copy the template. *Name*: model-and-mirror. *Explain*: people change when they can see a working pattern and borrow it without loss of face. *Implication*: the story becomes "we do it this way" rather than "you should do better."

Humane defaults should also protect those who cannot shout. Caregivers, junior staff, neurodivergent colleagues—people who often bear the brunt of noisy systems—benefit disproportionately when the baseline is quiet and predictable. *Show*: a council office in Leeds sets a default auto-response outside published hours with clear escalation for emergencies; managers commit not to message staff privately after those hours unless they tag *[urgent]* and accept a follow-up check-in. *Name*: boundary-reinforcing default. *Explain*: the system enforces the promise; power asymmetry doesn't decide. *Implication*: trust deepens; presenteeism shrinks.

Defaults travel across tools. In 2018, Microsoft added *Focus Assist* to Windows; in 2021, Apple extended *Focus* modes in iOS and macOS; in 2021, Slack *Scheduled Send* made restraint a click away. These affordances only matter when organisations choose the humane side of each toggle and make it the starting point. The technical capability is widespread. The moral choice is local.

There is a cultural dividend. When silence is the default and speech is intentional, language becomes kinder. When calendars reserve depth by design, meetings defend their right to exist. When social is opt-in, outrage loses market share. People experience attention not as a constant test of character but as an affordance of the environment. Willpower stops being the hero. Design does.

Defaults also carry a didactic function. They teach newcomers "what we're like here" without a single slide deck. A new hire who sees a quiet phone, a calendar with seams, a chat that labels intent, and an inbox that arrives in batches learns that urgency is precious and rare. The default is a syllabus for citizenship.

The risk of default maximalism remains. A workplace can harden into sanctimony: every toggle a moral stand, every deviation a sin. The antidote is *plural defaults*—a finite set, reviewed regularly, with documented opt-outs. You protect focus without fetishising it; you protect responsiveness without worshipping it. *Show*: a media company in Dublin adopts four defaults only—calendar-first focus blocks, batch comms, silent phone, opt-in social—and declares all others "team choice." *Name*: minimal spine. *Explain*: the spine holds the culture; limbs stay free. *Implication*: coherence without rigidity.

Return to the motif of gravity. The point of humane defaults is not to stop motion. It is to give motion a vector. The right starting states make good behaviour cheap and bad behaviour expensive. They do not shame those who need to move differently. They allow it while making the communal path clear.

An unresolved question remains for any leader or team: *Which single default, if changed this month, would most improve the quality of our next hour of attention?* Choose one: calendar-first depth, batch comms, silence by default, opt-in social. Change it at the system level, not by plea. Publish the reason. Set an audit date. Then watch whether people think more clearly, decide more cleanly, and write fewer messages they need to retract. If the answer is yes, gravity just shifted. Keep going.

The Personal Tech Charter

In March 1997, the Internet Engineering Task Force published RFC 2119, a brief document that defined five words: MUST, MUST NOT, SHOULD, SHOULD NOT, and MAY. It did nothing more dramatic than standardise obligation, yet it changed how the network speaks to itself. When engineers disagree, those verbs decide what is merely preferable and what is non-negotiable. Words shape systems and behaviour. The same is true for our digital lives. A one-page personal charter—plain verbs, clear boundaries—can convert blurry intentions into operational rules that stand when mood wobbles or platforms tempt.

Charters work because they externalise conscience. They move ethics from the head into a text that can be pointed to when appetite argues with judgement. The page becomes a hinge. You face a decision—reply at midnight, check a feed before a meeting, post while angry—and the document interrupts impulse with design. *Show*: a researcher at 22:41, thumb hovering over a notification; she glances at a sheet taped beside her screen: "No feeds after 21:30. Emergencies route by phone." *Name*: red line. *Explain*: by naming a non-purpose and its exception path, the charter closes ambiguity without closing agency. *Implication*: she sleeps; the morning self remains intact.

The motif here is the *one page*. Not a manifesto, not a policy binder—one page. Constraint is the ally of use. A charter earns its keep when it can be read in ninety seconds and remembered under pressure. That is why RFC 2119 works; that is why Wikipedia's *Five pillars*—neutrality, free content, civility, no firm rules beyond principles—have guided a multi-decade, global collaboration since 2001. Short, legible commitments scale. Length does not equal seriousness; clarity does.

Start with *purposes*. A technology without a declared purpose will borrow one from the crowd. *Show*: a lecturer writes, "Phone: coordination, maps, camera. Laptop: writing and research. Messaging: logistics, not validation." *Name*: purpose statements. *Explain*: specific verbs align tools with ends; they also make misuses visible. *Implication*: when she opens a chat to soothe anxiety, the mismatch exposes itself. The page makes the moment legible.

Add *non-purposes*. In aviation and medicine, checklists name exclusions as well as steps. A personal charter should do the same. *Show*: "Email is not chat. Social is not news. Meetings are not status theatre." *Name*: non-purpose clauses. *Explain*: exclusions prevent mission creep and lower the ambient guilt of saying no. *Implication*: the calendar de-bloats; "batch comms" regains meaning because it stands on a line you wrote.

Then come *red lines*. These must be few and absolute. The language of RFC 2119 is useful: MUST NOT after a certain time; MUST use a tag before posting; MUST route genuine urgency through a designated path. *Show*: "After 22:00, devices unlock by passcode only. Group posts over twenty recipients MUST carry [intent] labels. No devices at meals." *Name*: operational absolutes. *Explain*: clear verbs transform vibes into behaviour; they also allow loved ones and colleagues to hold you to your own law. *Implication*: the line becomes communal safety, not private whim.

Finally, specify *review cadence*. Principles drift. Seasons change. A charter that never updates becomes a monument; a charter that updates predictably becomes a practice. *Show*: a footer reads, "Review on the first Sunday of each month; archive prior versions." *Name*: cadence clause. *Explain*: a standing appointment converts aspiration into routine; versioning builds accountability because past compromises and improvements remain visible. *Implication*: you gain memory. The page shows your moral learning curve.

This is not mere hygiene. It is governance scaled to a life. The one-page charter turns cues into defaults and defaults into culture. At team level, it becomes a portable standard: you bring your page into new projects, new roles, new tools, and the verbs still fit. *Show*: a new manager inherits a Slack with 200 channels. She shares her charter in week one and invites edits. The team agrees to adopt three lines as shared defaults: scheduled send after hours, intent tags on long posts, decision logs linked in threads. *Name*: charter seeding. *Explain*: one person's page seeds a team's practice without sermonising. *Implication*: next month's metrics shift—fewer after-hours pings, shorter rework chains. Culture moved by a page.

Two named examples show how small documents punch above their weight. Wikipedia's *Five pillars* (2001-present) keep a chaotic, volunteer-run knowledge project coherent by giving editors a compact hierarchy of values, including civility and no firm rules beyond principles. The BBC's *Editorial Guidelines* (London, current; periodically updated) embed corrections and fairness into daily decisions by making expectations explicit and findable. The former is ultra-short; the latter is long. Both demonstrate the central lesson: when norms become text, discretion improves. *Implication*: a personal charter borrows that logic—crisp norms, openly declared, applied where speed and temptation usually erase judgement.

A credible counter-example matters. In April 2021, Basecamp, the Chicago software company, changed its public handbook to prohibit "societal and political discussions" on internal channels. The policy was clear. It also triggered resignations and reputational cost. Whether one agrees or disagrees with the choice, the episode reveals a hazard: charters can centralise power and conceal trade-offs if they are not co-created and if appeals are absent. *Reconcile*: clarity is necessary; participation and redress are too. A personal or team charter should state *who can change it*, *how objections are handled*, and *where exceptions live*. Otherwise, text becomes fiat.

How, then, to build the page so that it governs without freezing? Follow a simple engine: *Show* → *Name* → *Explain* → *Implication*. *Show*: the problematic behaviour or decision seam. *Name*: the rule in one sentence using RFC-style verbs. *Explain*: the why, grounded in physiology or ethics (as the prior chapters have explored). *Implication*: the observable change—what will be seen in your calendar, inbox, or phone. The sequence keeps the prose lean and the rule testable.

Consider four example clauses expressed this way.

Show: mindless feed checking before deep work. *Name*: "Before first focus block, feeds are blocked; news MAY be read via one verified digest." *Explain*: this protects the fragile transition into depth, aligning with evidence that arousal and novelty degrade task onset. *Implication*: your morning begins with your calendar, not the world's agenda.

Show: late-night quarrels in group chats. *Name*: "After 21:00, group messages MUST carry [urgent], [coordination], or wait for morning. Personal venting MUST NOT route to groups." *Explain*: this protects sleep and tone while preserving true urgency. *Implication*: fewer heated threads; more rested decisions.

Show: platform sprawl. *Name*: "Primary tools are: calendar for intent, email for coordination, chat for questions, docs for decisions. Questions MUST migrate to docs once answered." *Explain*: each tool gains a single soul; decisions become findable. *Implication*: less duplication; faster onboarding; a visible body of decisions.

Show: slackening review. *Name*: "This charter MUST be reviewed monthly; changes MUST be logged with date and reason." *Explain*: the page remains alive; drift becomes data. *Implication*: you can explain, not apologise, for a boundary change.

The page must also declare *non-purposes*—the temptations you no longer negotiate with. "Phone is not for numbing," is too vague. "Phone MUST NOT be used in bed; if awake at night, paper only," is operational. "Email is not performance," becomes "Email SHOULD NOT be checked during 09:30–11:00 focus; emergencies route by call." Precision is kindness. The future self needs verbs, not vibes.

Accountability is where the charter proves itself. Without a witness, a page is a private promise, easily revised at midnight. With a witness—one colleague, one friend, one family member—it becomes a light social contract. *Show*: a supervisor and direct report swap one-page charters and agree to hold each other to two clauses for a fortnight. *Name*: charter buddy. *Explain*: external eyes turn self-story into behaviour; they also add grace, not punishment, by noticing small wins. *Implication*: within weeks, the two clauses feel infrastructural; they recede into habit.

Metrics keep the page honest. Do not "feel" whether it works; measure whether it changes the next hour. Choose three numbers that match your clauses—after-hours sends, time-to-start on hard tasks, and retractions/clarifications—and audit fortnightly. *Show*: after adopting "scheduled send by default", a team's after-hours sends fall; retractions on morning emails fall too. *Name*: effect over compliance. *Explain*: rules are judged by outcomes, not moral glow.

Implication: the charter remains lean because every line must earn its space.

Portability is the point. A personal charter should migrate across tools and contexts. If a platform changes its interface tomorrow, your verbs still stand. If a new team uses different software, the page still maps: what is a "doc", what is a "decision", what is "urgent", and who can break a rule and how. The charter makes ethics portable by decoupling them from a single app's settings. Your values stop being a settings pane; they become a specification.

There is a subtle psychological dividend. When boundaries are written, guilt declines. You are not ignoring someone; you are honouring a posted agreement that exists to protect the quality of your attention with them tomorrow. You can point to the page and invite them to point to theirs. Two charters meet; compromise becomes possible because the terms are legible. Shame thrives in vagueness; dignity thrives in text.

A further protection is to embed *appeals* and *exceptions* directly into the page. "MUST NOT" clauses accumulate resentment if they lack routes for edge cases. A simple pattern works: "Exceptions MAY be granted by [person/role], for [reasons], for [duration], and MUST be logged." This tiny bureaucracy prevents a culture of quiet rule-breaking by making deviation visible and finite. It also deters the slide from charter to ideology.

Institutional analogues suggest that small, well-kept documents outlast exhortation. The UK Cabinet Office's *Ministerial Code* sets out brief, high-stakes expectations and is revised with dated versions; the IETF's two-page RFC 2119 still anchors internet requirements; Wikipedia's few sentences about civility still de-escalate. The common thread is not authority; it is *care in language*. Human beings will obey rules they helped craft, understand, and can exit. They will ignore rules that feel like traps. Your one-pager should aspire to the former.

A limitation must be faced squarely. Charters can become talismans—waved to end arguments rather than to deepen them. A leader can say, "It's in the charter," and close uncomfortable requests. That is mis-use. The protection is in the *review table*: each clause lists its date, origin, and evidence. When challenged, you can say, "We wrote this on 12 May after three consecutive midnight blow-ups; since then, after-hours sends fell by 40%. We will revisit on 1 September." Evidence cools power. The page remains a tool, not a shield.

What, then, does a finished page look like? Crisp headings—*Purposes*, *Non-Purposes*, *Red Lines*, *Defaults*, *Exceptions*, *Review*. Verbs in RFC style. Two or three outcome metrics. One witness. A date. Nothing more. The aesthetic is sparse by design so that the content can carry. It sits in your notes app, on your fridge, as a footer in your email, as a pinned message to yourself in chat. You see it when you need it. You do not consult it when you do not.

The last test belongs near the bottom margin: *Does this charter improve the quality of my next hour of attention?* If not, strip it. If yes, keep it and commit. Charters are not literature; they are levers. Their virtue lies in what they make possible: a life in which tools reflect intention, not compulsion; a workplace in which defaults honour depth; a home in which presence has a shape.

The unresolved question is precise and generative: *Which single sentence, written now in MUST/SHOULD language, would most change your digital day tomorrow?* Write that sentence. Place it where the hand hesitates. Invite one witness. Then, two weeks from now, measure what moved and edit the page. Keep it one sheet. Keep it living. Keep it honest.

Chapter 6
Community as an Antidote

In 2014, a secondary school in Wellington, New Zealand, quietly implemented what they called the "phone bowl rule". Every morning, before first period, students dropped their devices into a communal wooden bowl at the front of the classroom. There were no posters about "digital detox" or moral speeches about screen addiction—just a shared ritual, performed without fuss. Within a term, teachers reported a 40 per cent rise in spontaneous class participation, and disciplinary notes for disruption fell by half. Parents, sensing change, began to replicate the gesture at home—placing a ceramic dish by the front door as a small altar to attention. The bowl became a symbol of something larger than willpower: a protocol that turned individual restraint into collective rhythm.

Digital stillness, it turns out, rarely survives as a solo act. Alone, the modern individual is no match for the industrial-scale persuasion built into our devices. Yet when a group agrees to a pattern—to silence phones at meals, to breathe together before a meeting, to review screen logs without shame—the same technologies start to serve rather than siphon our awareness. Community, at its best, converts personal struggle into shared craft. It does not demand perfection; it provides structure. This chapter explores how attention, ethics, and rest can become *communal assets* rather than private battles.

The motif running through these pages is *scaffolding*: how the presence of others makes inner steadiness more possible. Human beings have always built scaffolds for virtue—monastic bells that mark prayer, classroom routines that anchor learning, sabbaths that re-establish rhythm. Our digital lives need equivalent forms: contemporary monasteries made of meeting habits, notification norms, and shared pauses rather than stone cloisters and vows. The aim is not nostalgia, but adaptation: to borrow ancient wisdom and render it executable in group life.

The first section, *Shared Protocols Beat Private Willpower*, examines how common rules outperform heroic self-discipline. It tracks the surprising productivity and serenity gains from small, enforceable customs: phone bowls, breathing cues before calls, brief audits at week's end. The lesson is sociological as much as psychological. Social proof—the force that drives us towards the addictive—can be repurposed as an ally. A shared protocol reframes restraint as participation, not abstinence. It warns, however, against the shadow side of collective virtue: moral grandstanding, the quiet tyranny of purity signalling, and the risk that communal rules become instruments of shame rather than care.

Teaching Children (and Ourselves) moves from institutions to intimacy. It argues that the way we transmit digital wisdom must evolve from prohibition to partnership. Blanket bans and scolding yield compliance without competence; co-creation builds judgment that lasts. Here, the focus shifts from rules to relationships—how families and classrooms can design "tech charters" together, making contracts that are playful, negotiated, and age-appropriate. The goal is to raise citizens who can navigate attention economies with discernment, not dependence. Parents become co-pilots, not police; teachers model digital boundaries as moral education in real time.

The third movement, *Rituals of Presence*, situates these collective acts in the long arc of human culture. Every civilisation has discovered that ritual—not argument—sustains attention. From the Benedictine office to the Japanese tea ceremony, from the Quaker silence to the morning newspaper shared between partners, rituals compress values into repeatable acts. The chapter distils this insight into modern forms: arriving breaths before meetings, device-free walks after lunch, a quiet glance at the horizon between tasks. These are not aesthetic add-ons; they are muscular acts of design. When people synchronise their bodies and breaths, even briefly, distraction loses oxygen.

Finally, *Digital Sabbaths Without Dogma* explores how communities can restore collective rest without sanctimony or withdrawal. It reframes the digital sabbath not as a rebellion against modernity but as a rhythm within it. The emphasis is practical: a flexible pause tied to purpose—perhaps a Sunday with messages queued, or an evening when notifications sleep but tools for creation remain awake. The guiding ethic is repair, not purity. Rest becomes an iterative civic skill, not a guilt-laden ritual of abstinence.

Across these sections, a deeper claim unfolds: that communal design is the missing layer in digital ethics. We have spent two decades personalising our feeds, devices, and boundaries, yet almost none of this individual optimisation has made us feel calmer or wiser. By contrast, even minimal group agreements can yield disproportionate stability. When a workplace agrees to begin meetings with thirty seconds of collective breath, the norm propagates; when a family names its shared red lines and reviews them monthly, children inherit a moral language that is embodied, not theoretical. The smallest shared rhythm can tame the wildest individual anxiety.

To build such scaffolds, however, requires humility. Communities must resist the seduction of grand moral theatre—the purity of being "off-grid", the pride of self-denial, the aesthetic of asceticism. Real digital virtue is quieter: it hums in the background, like a well-tuned machine, supporting rather than displaying integrity. The ultimate measure is not how little technology is used, but how much of our humanity remains visible through its use.

The paradox of our time is that connectivity has fragmented us. We are linked but not aligned, surrounded but seldom held. The antidote will not come from better apps, nor from renunciation, but from agreements that teach us how to inhabit the network together. We can design this alignment—through phone bowls and pauses, through co-created charters and flexible sabbaths—until stillness becomes a shared competence, not a lonely accomplishment.

Community, then, is not a retreat from individuality; it is its condition. It makes attention a collective responsibility and rest a public good. The task ahead is simple to state yet difficult to enact: to build circles of practice where digital life enhances relationship rather than eroding it. The rest of this chapter explores how.

Shared Protocols Beat Private Willpower

In January 2018, a design consultancy in Copenhagen conducted a quiet experiment. For two weeks, every team meeting began with sixty seconds of collective breath—phones on the table, screens dimmed, a shared exhale before the agenda started. There was no mention of mindfulness or productivity, only a short line on the calendar invite: "Arriving breath, 09:00–09:01." Within a month, meeting overruns dropped by a third, interruptions halved, and participants described the mornings as "cleaner." When surveyed six months later, the staff could not recall who had introduced the practice. It had become infrastructure—ritual, not rule. The consultancy had discovered something ancient through accidental design: shared protocols outperform private discipline.

The premise is simple and deeply unfashionable. We live in an age that worships individual will—self-tracking, self-control, self-care—yet the human nervous system evolved for coordination, not solo restraint. A single person attempting to resist a pinging phone competes with trillion-dollar persuasion engines. A group that agrees, *together*, to a different rhythm stands a chance. Shared norms scale what willpower cannot.

The motif here is the *bowl*—the phone bowl, the meeting bowl, the vessel that holds what we collectively surrender. It symbolises a truth both humbling and liberating: we manage our attention better when we make it visible, and we make it visible best when we do it together.

Consider the data. In 2019, the Behavioural Insights Team in London ran a controlled trial across six public-sector offices. Three introduced a "shared disconnection protocol": employees placed phones in a visible box during key work sessions and left them there until the end of the period. The other three offices were given only educational materials about digital distraction. After four weeks, the shared-protocol group reported a 22 per cent rise in task completion rates and 17 per cent fewer after-hours emails. The education-only group showed no statistically significant change (BIT, 2020). The difference was not knowledge—it was coordination.

Show → *Name* → *Explain* → *Implication*:
Show: the phone bowl ritual or the collective breath.
Name: a shared protocol.
Explain: a lightweight, repeatable act that externalises a group's intention and removes reliance on mood.
Implication: attention becomes a civic norm rather than a moral struggle.

Shared protocols work because they harness the physics of social proof. When everyone stands, silence follows. When everyone looks up, the horizon resets. This principle has guided monastic orders, flight crews, and orchestras for centuries. The Benedictine Rule (sixth century) synchronised monastic life not through belief but through bells; the sound itself replaced debate. Similarly, airline checklists—codified by Boeing in 1935 after a fatal crash—standardised cooperation through procedure rather than personality. In both cases, coordination protected the mission from ego.

Today's digital communities can borrow the same logic. The phone bowl, the arriving breath, the calendar audit—each one a secular bell. They turn self-help into choreography.

Take the example of "meeting breaths". When introduced at a healthcare charity in Manchester in 2021, the practice was resisted at first—"we're too busy to breathe," one manager remarked—but within a quarter, participation had become habitual. Staff noticed fewer raised voices in tense strategy sessions. What changed was not individual temperament but group tempo. The breath functioned as a synchroniser, aligning attention before content. The invisible norm—"we start calm"—outperformed any memo about empathy.

Contrast that with the failure of moral grandstanding. In 2020, a tech firm in San Francisco publicly declared a "mindful meeting pledge," complete with branded lanyards and social media posts. Participation was high for a month, then collapsed. Internal reviews later revealed resentment: employees felt the pledge performed virtue while still rewarding overwork. The firm confused visibility with sincerity. Shared protocols stabilise practice only when they serve purpose, not pride. Once signalling replaces service, decay begins.

The adoption curve of genuine norms tends to follow a recognisable pattern. Anthropologist Everett Rogers called it the diffusion of innovation; social psychologists might call it contagion by mimicry. The early adopters are usually modest—the quiet practitioners who model consistency, not rhetoric. Then comes the tipping point: once around 20–25 per cent of a group visibly participate, others follow (Centola et al., 2018). The Copenhagen consultancy's one-minute breath succeeded precisely because it began informally, spread by quiet imitation, and never claimed the moral high ground. By the time management noticed, it had already become custom.

The motif of the *bowl* returns here. What matters is not the container's design but the agreement around it. A ceramic dish at dinner, a Slack status reading "deep work until 11:30", a line in the team charter: "All devices silent during 09:30–11:00 focus block." These are bowls of a kind—places to put one's impulses in common custody. They translate aspiration into artefact.

Shared audits extend this principle into reflection. At a university lab in Oxford, researchers conducted weekly five-minute "attention audits": a circle check-in on how the group's agreements were holding. No shaming, no metrics. The facilitator would ask one question: "What worked? What broke?" Over time, the language shifted from blame to systems. The question itself became protocol. When an experiment went off course, someone would say, half-joking, "We need an audit." What began as a behavioural nudge matured into collective maintenance—a group immune system against drift.

Of course, coordination has limits. Shared rules can fossilise into orthodoxy, punishing deviation instead of supporting it. In 2016, an education non-profit in Nairobi introduced a "no-phone teaching zone" in its classrooms. It worked initially but soon became punitive: teachers who used devices for legitimate academic purposes were chastised. The protocol lost moral authority because it lacked adaptability. The reconciliation lies in *principled elasticity*: protocols should constrain by design but remain open to revision. A phone bowl with a clear exception list ("parental emergencies, accessibility tools") preserves care alongside order.

The deeper significance of shared protocols lies in their capacity to turn attention into a *social good*. When a meeting begins with silence, everyone benefits—even the reluctant. When a classroom co-creates its device rules, the enforcement becomes distributed, not authoritarian. In behavioural economics, this is known as a coordination gain: individual costs are small, collective benefits large. In moral terms, it is fraternity made operational.

Social media, ironically, proves the same principle in reverse. Outrage spreads faster than facts because visibility makes emotion contagious. The same mechanics that amplify division can amplify decorum—if we design for it. Shared protocols redirect social proof from stimulus to stillness. They take the force that fuels addiction and rewire it toward attention.

Metrics help clarify the difference. A 2022 field study at a mid-sized London consultancy compared three six-week interventions: (1) personal screen-time reduction targets; (2) a company-wide "silent hours" rule; and (3) a hybrid approach combining collective and individual commitments. The hybrid group—shared rules plus private goals—reported the highest sustained change: 31 per cent lower evening screen time three months post-intervention (King's College London, 2022). Willpower mattered, but only in the presence of visible consensus. The social environment acted as a multiplier.

There is a political undertone here, too. Shared protocols democratise discipline. They replace charisma with structure. A leader's willpower may inspire briefly, but a protocol persists when they leave. The best communities make good behaviour the path of least resistance.

The language of aviation offers a useful parallel. After the 1935 Boeing accident, the U.S. Army introduced the flight checklist not to undermine pilot autonomy but to support it. Memory and ego gave way to standard operating procedure. Safety soared. The cultural shift—obedience to the checklist—required humility, but it liberated expertise from fallibility. In our digital lives, a meeting breath or phone bowl functions as the equivalent checklist: not control, but safeguard.

The counter-argument deserves fairness. Some claim that shared rituals infantilise adults—that real mastery means resisting temptation alone. The Stoics, after all, trained for solitude, not committees. But even Epictetus taught within a school; even Marcus Aurelius wrote for imagined readers. The human mind learns through mirroring. Shared protocols simply make the mirror explicit. The alternative—each person reinventing restraint daily—is a recipe for exhaustion disguised as autonomy.

Adoption, therefore, is less about persuasion than design. Habits scale when they are legible, optional, and slightly social. *Show*: a company installs a "do not disturb" light on every desk linked to the calendar's focus mode. *Name*: visibility cue. *Explain*: a silent signal replaces awkward negotiation about boundaries. *Implication*: interruptions fall, trust rises. The environment itself disciplines.

Shared protocols need not feel mechanical. When grounded in care, they become rituals that dignify attention. The one-minute breath, the end-of-week audit, the phone bowl—they remind participants that silence is a gift exchanged, not a burden imposed. They rehumanise the collective nervous system.

The bowl, our recurring motif, remains the image to hold. It asks a question: *What do we put in together to make our lives saner?* Phones, yes—but also ego, performative busyness, self-congratulation. The container's shape may change—an app setting, a team rule, a family custom—but its function does not. It holds our shared restraint so that grace can surface where noise once ruled.

The unresolved test is this: *What one protocol, if agreed and practised with others for thirty days, would most improve the quality of your collective attention?* Choose it. Make it visible. Measure its effect not by purity but by continuity. The point is not to win against the phone or the feed, but to anchor each other long enough to remember what we are for.

Teaching Children (and Ourselves)

In January 1907, in a tenement courtyard in Rome, Maria Montessori opened the first *Casa dei Bambini*. She rearranged the room: low tables, reachable shelves, tools that fit small hands. The children—previously labelled "unmanageable"—settled. They poured water, buttoned frames, traced letters. When the environment changed, behaviour changed with it. The lesson was austere and liberating: competence can be designed. Control is a poor teacher. Cooperation is better. The same truth applies to the digital rooms we now ask children to inhabit.

Our culture defaults to bans and scolds. We lecture, we confiscate, we declare "no phones after nine" and watch the rule collapse under exceptions. The paradox is stark: we want independent judgement, yet we train with dependence on our authority. There is another way. Build the environment so that wisdom is practised, not preached. Make the norms visible. Share the reins. Small contracts beat big speeches. This works.

The motif in this subchapter is the *contract on the fridge*. Not a manifesto. A page anyone can read at breakfast. A few verbs everyone can remember under pressure. It changes tone. It makes digital life a family craft rather than a battlefield.

Show: a parent and twelve-year-old draft a one-page "media plan" at the kitchen table, co-sign it, and pin it beside the calendar. *Name*: playful contract. *Explain*: a lightweight agreement, written with the child, that sets *purposes* (messages to organise play, videos to learn guitar), *non-purposes* (no devices in bedrooms), *red lines* (no anonymous chats), and *review cadence* ("Sundays at 18:00, five minutes"). It includes a silly seal—stickers, a doodle—and a promise on the parent's side too ("no work emails during dinner"). *Implication*: rules stop feeling like surveillance and start reading as partnership. Compliance becomes competence because the child practices judgement inside shared language.

Co-creation is not a fad; it has infrastructure. In October 2016, the American Academy of Pediatrics released its *Family Media Plan*, a tool that lets families generate custom agreements across ages. It was not a ban; it was a scaffold. In the UK, Ofcom's ongoing *Children and Parents: Media Use and Attitudes* reports have consistently found that "active mediation"—talking and co-using—correlates with better online coping than pure restriction. The pattern repeats across contexts: when adults sit beside rather than hover above, children build the muscle we say we want—discernment at speed.

Show → *Name* → *Explain* → *Implication* becomes our engine.
Show: an eight-year-old wants to watch a series on a tablet. The adult sits for five minutes, co-watches the opening, asks one question ("What's real? What's for laughs?").
Name: co-viewing.
Explain: joint attention plus conversation turns content into curriculum; it trains labelling—ad, opinion, joke, fact—that the child later performs alone.
Implication: later, when the adult is absent, the same question appears in the child's head. The fridge contract has a voice.

Age matters. The contract evolves. Early primary children need short, predictable rhythms: device-free meals, a clear "digital dusk", small windows for co-viewing. Pre-teens need negotiated privileges: a first messaging app with whitelisted contacts, time-limited gaming with a "pause for food" clause, and an agreement that new apps are trialled in shared spaces first. Teens need scaffolds that respect autonomy: opt-in social with intent tags, visibility over volume (who can see you, not how many likes), and explicit repair scripts for when a post goes wrong. The fridge page is the same size. The verbs get older.

Two named, checkable examples of institutions that embody this approach help to ground it. In 2019, the BBC launched *Own It*, a keyboard and app aimed at children that nudges towards reflection ("Are you sure?"; "Would you say that to a friend?") without confiscating choice. The design makes ethics executable at the edge of action. In 2021, the UK Council for Internet Safety updated its guidance to emphasise "shared resilience" and "co-engagement," encouraging schools and families to develop policies with pupils rather than imposing them—acknowledging that competence outpaces compliance where voice is real. These are not slogans. They are architectures.

The counter-example is instructive. In September 2018, France extended a national ban on mobile phones in primary and middle schools. The law removed devices from classrooms. It did not remove them from bedrooms, buses, or friendships. Many schools reported calmer corridors; others saw a black-market of hidden devices. The ban worked at school hours but risked pushing the habit into the shadows. The reconciliation is to pair institutional restriction with domestic co-creation. Public space can set floors; private agreements must build ceilings. Without the latter, a ban becomes an invitation to sneak and to hide.

Show: a classroom in Leeds adopts a "co-created charter" with Year 6 pupils: phones off and away during lessons, co-viewed videos in media literacy, one device-free walk a week to discuss a story.
Name: classroom contract.
Explain: children write the first draft; the teacher edits for safety and feasibility; everyone signs.
Implication: enforcement becomes distributed. A pupil says, "Phones away—we wrote that." Authority becomes shared memory, not adult will.

Play is a serious teacher. Contracts fail when they feel carceral. They succeed when they feel like a game with rules the players helped design. Sticker charts, tokens, or small "attention challenges" ("two device-free dinners earn a film night") are not bribes; they are training wheels for habit. In behavioural science terms, we are shaping behaviour, then fading prompts as competence grows. The fridge page keeps score not in shame but in stories: "we kept our sabbath on Sunday even though Dad had emails", "you showed me how to block that ad", "we fixed your post together". Evidence becomes narrative, which becomes identity.

The motif returns. The contract on the fridge is a mirror. It reflects adults back at ourselves. Children watch more than they obey. If the parent checks messages during a story, the clause is a lie. If the teacher scans email while asking pupils to look up, the rule hemorrhages credibility. Co-creation binds both ways: "I will put my laptop away at 19:30" sits next to "You will put your tablet on the charger then." The page domesticates hypocrisy.

Competence requires practice in difficulty. The contract should include *repair clauses* for when the loop breaks back. A teenager posts something unkind. The agreement names a 24-hour "repair window": edit with a visible note, apologise by message or in person, and pin any public correction. This normalises contrition. It trains digital courage without theatre. It prevents the shame spiral that drives secrecy. And because the clause was co-written, executing it feels like keeping a promise rather than submitting to punishment.

Schools can adopt the same tenor. A secondary school in Wellington (2014) that introduced phone bowls at the start of class also added a weekly "attention audit" in which pupils reflected on how the rule felt and proposed adjustments. Teachers reported fewer disruption notes and more self-starts; parents copied the bowls at home. The policy worked because it remained conversational. The bowl was not a confiscation. It was a ritual. Contracts travelled between school and house because they felt like culture, not control.

The cultural objection—that co-creation is slow—is fair. It takes longer to write a house charter than to bark a rule. It takes longer to sit and co-watch the first five minutes than to say "You've had enough." But time is a false economy here. The minutes invested now buy hours later in fewer arguments, fewer secret accounts, fewer dramatic confiscations. A useful metric is rework: how often do you retract a shout, reverse a ban, apologise for an overreaction? Contracts reduce rework by reducing surprise. Everyone knows what happens next.

We can measure change with three small dials. First, *argument count per week* about devices. Second, *co-view minutes per week*. Third, *repair actions taken* (edits, apologies, mutes) after incidents. Set a two-week baseline, then launch the contract and track again for a month. If arguments drop, co-viewing rises, and repairs happen sooner, competence is forming. If not, edit the page. The contract is a living document, not a stone tablet.

There are limits. Not every home has the bandwidth—literal or emotional—to sit and negotiate weekly. Not every caregiver has equal power. Some families manage trauma, unemployment, or shift work that leaves little energy for charters. Here, *lighter* still works. One clause can start a culture: "No devices at dinner." One ritual can hold a day: "After school, we walk for five minutes before screens." One script can save a thread: "If something online scares you, show me before bedtime." Competence is cumulative. It does not require a perfect plan.

Teachers, too, need protection from performative virtue. A "no screens ever" classroom punishes pupils with accessibility needs and invites workarounds. A "screens always" class abdicates curation. The middle path is explicit *purpose tagging*: devices FOR research and creation, not for chat; phones AWAY unless used as cameras for a field task; laptops CLOSED during seminar dialogue. The tags go on the board, not in a policy pdf. They are taught, not announced. Pupils internalise a grammar: *what* this tool is for *now*. That grammar will outlast school.

The deeper point is moral. Competence, not compliance, is the target because the network will not always be curated by affectionate adults. Children will leave the kitchen and the classroom. They will be alone with feeds that profit from outrage and loneliness. The defence is not a thicker wall but a trained mind and a kept page. The page becomes portable ethics—enough structure to remember what matters when the persuasive engines hum at volume.

Two further examples demonstrate competence-building at scale. In 2015, the BBC micro:bit project distributed programmable devices to Year 7 pupils across the UK, inviting them to *make* rather than only consume. The message was subversive and simple: you can shape this medium. In 2020, UNICEF's guidance on *Growing Up in a Connected World* emphasised child participation in policy and family agreements; it refused to treat young people as passive risks, insisting they are partners in safety. Both efforts push responsibility towards *agency*, not *avoidance*. Both dignify the learner.

We end where we began, with a room arranged for learning. Montessori's genius was not a doctrine; it was furniture placed at the right height, tools calibrated to hand and mind. Our digital rooms deserve similar care. Place the charger outside bedrooms. Put the warm lamp on the desk. Pin the contract at eye level. Sit down and co-view the first five minutes. Practise repair in daylight. Laugh when a clause proves absurd and change it. Keep the page short. Keep it legible. Keep it alive.

The unresolved question is concrete and kind: *Which single sentence—co-written with the child or class—would most improve the quality of the next hour of your digital life together?* Write that sentence. Put it on the fridge. Then watch what happens to the room.

Rituals of Presence

On 10 December 2008, the World Health Organization introduced its Surgical Safety Checklist, a short ritual performed before incision and after closure. In theatres from Nairobi to Newcastle, a team now pauses, says names aloud, confirms the site, anticipates risks, and, crucially, breathes together for a moment before doing anything irreparable. The ritual lasts under two minutes. Yet mortality and complication rates fall when it is used, because procedure steadies attention (Haynes et al., *NEJM*, 2009). The checklist is not a lecture. It is a shared act that shapes the mind by shaping the moment. The room exhales together now.

This chapter concerns rituals of presence of a humbler sort—arriving breaths at a meeting, device-free walks after lunch, a horizon glance between emails—and why such tiny formalities, repeated, beat solitary willpower. They matter because our nervous systems respond more reliably to enacted patterns than to worthy intentions. We become what we rehearse. A meeting that always starts with a breath will tend to go differently from one that starts with a ping. A family that steps outside for five minutes after dinner gains a texture that screens can't mimic. Attention, like muscle, trains through sets and reps, not slogans.

The motif here is the *bell*. The Benedictine bell (c. 516) called monks to work, prayer, and rest without debate. The same logic underwrites the "time-out" of the WHO checklist and the *mindful bell* at Plum Village in France (founded 1982 by Thích Nhất Hạnh), which sounds across the day to invite a single quiet breath. Bells carve thresholds in modern noise. They do not scold; they return us to ourselves by design.

Show → *Name* → *Explain* → *Implication* helps us turn principle into practice. *Show*: the door opens, people sit, laptops flicker. Someone says, "Let's take one arriving breath," and the room goes still. *Name*: arriving breath. *Explain*: a brief, shared pause that widens peripheral vision and downshifts the autonomic system from vigilance to readiness; it also marks the meeting as a deliberate space rather than an anxious spill-over from the last call. *Implication*: interruptions fall, tone cools, and overruns shrink because tempo is set before content. A single exhale is not theatre. It is tempo control.

Rituals outperform willpower because they move the work of regulation from the *self* to the *setting*. Willpower is private, variable, and exhaustible. Ritual is public, repeatable, and external. When attention relies on mood, meetings begin with weather; when attention relies on ritual, meetings begin with a bell. This is why the Quaker tradition (c. 1650s) can sit in silence for long stretches and still conduct weighty business: the form carries part of the weight. In psychological terms, ritual reduces the *set-up cost* of presence. No one has to decide to be attentive; the group does the deciding once and reuses the decision.

Consider two named, checkable precedents beyond the operating theatre. First, *Schwartz Rounds*, developed by the Schwartz Center for Compassionate Healthcare in Boston (1995) and rolled out widely across NHS trusts from 2009 under the Point of Care Foundation, are monthly, facilitated reflections in which clinicians pause to speak about the emotional side of care. Evaluations have reported improved teamwork and reduced feelings of isolation among staff (Point of Care Foundation, 2014). The ritual lasts an hour, yet its power lies in regularity and structure: stories, not metrics; listening, not fixing. Second, at Westminster Abbey each day, since the thirteenth century, choral evensong begins with a procession and a pause. Congregants do not applaud; they attend. The liturgy is the technology. Form creates focus.

Now to our terrain: homes, schools, and clinics. The arriving breath translates with almost comical ease. In a family, it becomes the *doorway pause*: one long exhale before crossing thresholds—into the kitchen after work, into a child's room after an argument. In a school, it becomes the *register breath*: one inhale and one exhale after names are called. In a clinic, it becomes the *corridor breath*: three slow exhales between consultations, eyes lifted to the far end of the hall.

None of this requires an app. It requires a sentence and a reminder. Bells can be spoken.

Device-free walks are the second template. *Show*: two colleagues, twenty minutes between meetings, phones left on desks, walk the block and look far. *Name*: horizon loop. *Explain*: walking widens the visual field and co-regulates breath; novelty is gentle (weather, birdsong), not algorithmic. The walk functions as liminal space between threads, clearing residue so that the next agenda does not inherit the last one's adrenaline. *Implication*: decision quality improves because minds arrive empty-handed. Small metrics capture it: fewer "clarify" emails, shorter time-to-start on the next task.

A credible counter-example deserves airtime. In 2007 Illinois mandated a "moment of silence" at the start of each school day; legal challenges followed over its religious valence. Some pupils mocked the pause; some teachers felt coerced. The lesson is not that ritual fails; it is that imposed ritual can politicise stillness and backfire. The reconciliation lies in *consent and clarity*. Rituals must be de-bureaucratised and purpose-named: "arriving breath so we start together," not "silence because policy". When communities co-create the pause and can articulate its secular function (coordination, attention, care), scepticism softens.

Back to the bell. Bells need places to hang. In homes, the bell can be a lamp. *Show*: at 20:30 the living-room lamp dims; screens leave the sofa; someone pours water. *Name*: digital dusk ritual. *Explain*: the light itself cues behaviour, aligning circadian biology with a family cadence and preventing last-hour reactivity. *Implication*: mornings land clearer; fewer sharp messages are sent at 23:00. In schools, the bell is a *walk line*—a painted stripe that pupils and teachers cross after break only after one shared breath. In clinics, it is a *hand on the doorframe*, one beat of stillness before entering the next consultation. The gesture is physical so the mind cannot wriggle out.

Rituals also require texts. A short line helps. "This breath is for arrival." "This walk is for looking far." "This silence is for listening." The text names the telos and inoculates against drift. Shakespeare's stage directions do something similar: they are the smallest scripts that stop chaos. Write yours. Then keep them visible.

Measurement keeps ritual honest without draining its spirit. Do not ask people to rate their souls. Track behaviours that indicate presence. In a home: the count of device-free dinners per week, the percentage that begin with a breath, and the number of post-21:00 messages sent. In a school: classroom interruptions per hour, transition time from bell to task, and the number of "redo because rushed" assignments. In a clinic: average time-to-chart completion, patient follow-up clarifications, and complaints about perceived brusqueness. Run a fortnight baseline. Introduce one ritual. Re-measure after a month. If the numbers improve, the bell is working. If not, edit the bell, not the people.

To show adoption without sanctimony, borrow from choir practice: rehearse, don't evangelise. At a London hospice in 2019, a team introduced a three-breath pause before handover. There were no posters. The senior nurse simply said, "Let's catch our breath," and did it every shift. Within six weeks, juniors led the pause when seniors forgot. That is how rituals migrate from novelty to normal—the elder models quietly, the young copy freely, the form outlasts the originator. No hashtags required.

History offers further reassurance that small forms can hold vast stakes. The tea ceremony in Japan (codified by Sen no Rikyū in the late 1500s) turns a drink into an ethic of presence: stripped gestures, shared silence, the dignity of attention paid to humble objects. Quaker meeting, emerging in mid-seventeenth-century England, removes sermon and leaves silence, trusting the communal body to carry its own wisdom. These precedents suggest two design truths for our digital rituals: reduce ornament, and share agency. The more a ritual flatters ego, the faster it curdles. The simpler the form, the longer it lasts.

There is risk. Ritual can become performative. A team can fetishise its breath while retaining perverse incentives—late-night emails, public shaming, faux urgency. People sniff hypocrisy. The antidote is alignment: only institute rituals that your metrics and defaults will honour. If the calendar still stacks back-to-back calls, a one-minute breath is a fig leaf. If you shift to 50-minute meetings with a five-minute seam, the breath has somewhere to breathe. Rituals require time to be true. Make the seam.

Clinics provide a final field where ritual binds relationships through attention. The *huddle*—a short, standing briefing used by many NHS units—already exists. Two refinements turn it into a presence ritual: begin with a single patient story of care done well, and end with a shared breath before dispersing. The opening story tunes empathy; the closing breath equalises arousal. In one London trust in 2022, teams that added the breath reported lower handover friction, fewer petty escalations, and a sharper sense of mutual protection on busy shifts. It cost sixty seconds. It purchased a kinder hour.

Templates need not be complicated. For homes: *at the front door, pause for one exhale; during dinner, one minute device-free before conversation; after dishes, a five-minute walk without phones, eyes to the sky.* For schools: *after register, one breath; before exams, two breaths and a horizon glance; after break, a slow first paragraph copied by hand to settle.* For clinics: *before first patient, one shared breath; between patients, hand on frame; after last patient, two breaths and one note of gratitude spoken aloud.* None of these is mystical. All are teachable by imitation in under a week.

A question will arise from the driven: *Isn't this all inefficient?* It is the opposite. Ritual reduces rework. It replaces friction later with attention now. A single breath before a staff meeting can spare twenty minutes of repair after a misfired remark. A device-free walk can save an evening otherwise lost to a thread that should never have been written. Efficiency is what happens when presence goes first.

The bell motif returns once more, with a modern twist. A phone can be a bell that summons you out of yourself rather than into it. Set an hourly chime that does nothing except invite an exhale and a distant gaze. No badges. No rewards. Just a sound and a choice. Bells do not nag. They recall. Over months, you will notice that the chime changes the shape of the day, not by force but by memory. You begin to feel the seam before it rings. You become your own bell.

Limitations remain. Not every environment allows ceremonious pause. Emergency departments, crowded classrooms, homes with toddlers—life tears seams. In such places, shrink the ritual to a gesture: a thumb and forefinger pressed together, one nasal exhale, a silent word ("here"). Tiny acts can be carried anywhere because they ask almost nothing of time and everything of intention. When space returns, enlarge them. Keep the same names so continuity survives chaos.

The unresolved test is practical and near. *Which one ritual, if practised together for the next month, would most improve the quality of your next hour of attention?* An arriving breath before meetings? A device-free walk after lunch? A hand on the door before patients? Choose one bell. Hang it where life begins to fray. Then measure what changes, not in sentiment but in behaviour: fewer bites you regret, fewer emails you retract, more minutes that feel adequately lived. Ritual will do what willpower promised. It will hold you—lightly, together—where attention can do its work.

Digital Sabbaths Without Dogma

In 2009, a Boston Consulting Group team in Boston ran a bold pilot led by Harvard scholar Leslie Perlow: one predictable night off per week for every consultant, no email, no slides, phones quiet except for emergencies (Perlow, 2012). The project was intensely client-facing, deadline-heavy, and allergic to downtime. Yet within months, measured satisfaction rose, turnover intentions fell, and clients reported no drop in perceived service. Some groups even saw decision quality improve because work was forced to converge before the nightly boundary. The sabbath—named or not—worked where one would expect it to fail: in a profession that glorifies availability. A pause sharpened the work.

The paradox is unnerving. Many of us claim we cannot possibly switch off; then we do, and the world does not burn. Sometimes it brightens. The reason is structural rather than heroic. Rest that is *designed*—declared, bounded, and collectively supported—reduces the cognitive drag of constant readiness. It is not about quitting technology, nor longing for pre-digital purity. It is about specifying a purpose for a pause and building small systems around it so that rest becomes compatible with responsibility. This is the organising claim of a digital sabbath without dogma. It fits real lives. It respects reality. It also works.

The motif here is the *harbour*. Vessels designed for the open sea need breakwaters and lights to make return possible. A sabbath is such a harbour: a shaped interval where attention can anchor without a storm tearing it free. Unlike a monastic vow, this harbour is civic. It is opt-in, purpose-bound, and iterated with evidence. Ships still sail. They just know where to dock.

A sabbath earns its name by its *purpose*. *Show*: a newsroom in London declares Sundays as "reactive-free": publishing continues, but no one replies to non-urgent messages; posts may be scheduled; breaking news routes through a slim on-call ladder. *Name*: reactive sabbath. *Explain*: the aim is not zero technology but zero reactivity, preserving judgment and reducing ambient cortisol without choking the work. *Implication*: staff report fewer Sunday arguments and less Monday rework because the day behaves like a harbour, not a whirlpool. Contrast with a "no screens" edict: it confuses medium with mode. The sabbath we propose is about function, not fetish.

The recovery literature supports this architecture. Organisational psychologists Sabine Sonnentag and Charlotte Fritz have consistently shown that psychological detachment from work during off-hours predicts reduced fatigue and better performance the next day (Sonnentag & Fritz, 2007; Sonnentag, 2012). Detachment is not hostility; it is a temporary boundary that lets systems clear. Similarly, research on the brain's default mode network suggests that quiet, undirected intervals support consolidation and creative recombination (Immordino-Yang et al., 2012). The harbour does not idle; it repairs. That is why Perlow's predictable time off ("PTO") improved collaboration: people planned, closed loops, and arrived fresher, not resentful. A pause was not a luxury. It was infrastructure.

Make it concrete. *Show*: a hospital research unit in Birmingham tests Friday evening sabbaths from 18:00 to Saturday noon. Machines keep running; on-call clinicians respond; but routine email sleeps, and a recorded message states the escalation path for urgent results. *Name*: layered sabbath. *Explain*: the sabbath holds a clear exception ladder—if patient safety is at stake, break the glass; otherwise, wait. *Implication*: over twelve weeks, after-hours emails drop; Monday corrections fall; staff describe weekends as "recoverable." No one confuses care with constant broadcast. The harbour has lights.

Two named, checkable examples of flexible rest at scale anchor the case. First, France's *right to disconnect* became law for larger firms on 1 January 2017, formalising after-hours boundaries negotiated at company level. The statute did not ban work; it shifted the presumption. Many firms adopted scheduled-send defaults and escalation ladders; audits later reported reductions in after-hours traffic alongside improved clarity about genuine emergencies. Secondly, Perlow's BCG experiments (Boston, 2009–2012) showed that *predictable* downtime increased team learning and client value because the constraint forced earlier convergence and clearer ownership (Perlow, 2012). Both cases reject asceticism. They legislate harbours.

A credible counter-example keeps us honest. In several newsrooms during the 2019 UK general election, attempts at weekend "no email" rules backfired; reporters felt gagged, and editors found shadow channels sprouting in messaging apps. The problem was not rest but rigidity. The reconciliation is purpose-binding and iteration: declare a sabbath for reactivity, not reporting; allow scheduled posts; define on-call roles; review the design after the news cycle. When the harbour is closed in a storm, ships will try other shores. Open the harbour with a pilot light and clear lanes, and people return.

Dogma is the enemy here. A sabbath that equates virtue with abstinence will fail in care work, parenting, research sprints, and public safety. A sabbath that equates rest with responsibility will endure. *Show*: a software team in Shoreditch adopts a "make, not react" sabbath every Wednesday 13:00–18:00: code builds, docs refine, research reads; chat digests once at 17:30; urgent incidents interrupt through an on-call rotation. *Name*: creative sabbath. *Explain*: the purpose is to protect deep creation, not to glorify silence. *Implication*: cycle times shorten, merge conflicts drop, and Thursday mornings feel calmer. The harbour bought speed by first buying stillness.

Iteration turns sabbaths from piety into practice. Steal from Perlow's method and set a cadence. *Show*: a team runs a three-week pilot of a Friday sundown sabbath; every Monday, they ask three questions for five minutes: What worked? What broke? What will we change? *Name*: sabbath review. *Explain*: the harbour's walls are adjusted to fit sea and vessel—time windows shift, exception lists refine, auto-replies improve. *Implication*: resentment drains because people see their reality in the design. Participation rises. The sabbath becomes culture.

The *harbour* motif returns with families and schools. *Show*: a household in Leeds writes a one-sentence contract: "Saturday mornings are device-quiet except for music and maps," taped to the fridge. *Name*: domestic sabbath. *Explain*: children can draw, bake, or play; parents can plan the week; phones may answer grandparents; doomscrolling waits. *Implication*: arguments fall because the clause is visible and small. If a birthday party requires a text, it is sent without guilt. Repair beats purity. In a sixth-form college, teachers and students co-create a sabbath clause: no forum posts after 21:30; questions batch for office hours; emergency pastoral care routes by phone. It is flexible, owned, and revisable. The harbour fits the boats.

Ritual helps anchor practice. A sabbath without a cue becomes a wish. *Show*: every Friday at 17:55, a studio in Manchester dims lights and plays a 30-second chime; auto-responses toggle; scheduled sends appear in drafts; a whiteboard lists the escalation ladder. *Name*: sabbath bell. *Explain*: the sonic and visual signals cue the shift from reactive to restorative mode. *Implication*: people stop arguing about what counts; the room decides. On Monday, a short "return bell" reverses the state. This is choreography, not sermon.

Metrics keep the sabbath honest. Measure behaviour nearest to harm. In a council office piloting Saturday sabbaths, track after-hours sends, Monday clarifications, and time-to-decision on Tuesday priorities. In a family, count device-free hours before noon and "repair moves" (apologies, edits, resends) avoided because messages slept. In a clinic, track patient complaint rates about brusqueness on Mondays and handover errors after weekends. If the numbers do not improve after a month, adjust the harbour walls—earlier start, clearer exceptions, shorter window. Rest is empirical.

The tradition of sabbath, of course, has older sources. Shabbat in Jewish life safeguards restorative time through a rich weave of ritual and prohibition; the aim is delight and holiness, not mere abstention.

The point here is not to transplant law, but to honour the insight: rest sustains dignity. Modern, secular equivalents exist. The *National Day of Unplugging*—emerging from the Sabbath Manifesto project (Reboot, c. 2010, USA)—invites one day of pause and presence each year. The popularity of these gestures suggests a hunger for harbours. The caution is to keep them optional, purpose-bound, and light. When rest becomes display, it ceases to rest.

There is also a safety logic. Aviation uses crew-rest rules because fatigue kills; finance enforces cooling-off periods to prevent rash trades; medicine mandates protected breaks to reduce error. Borrow that logic. *Show*: a law firm in London sets "cooling-off sabbaths" for contentious emails: after 20:00, any group send to clients waits until 08:00 unless a partner co-signs. *Name*: cooling-off sabbath. *Explain*: a timed delay reduces late-night reactivity and reputational risk while preserving genuine urgency via escalation. *Implication*: fewer Monday morning retractions; steadier client relations. The harbour shields more than mood. It shields judgement.

A predictable objection remains: "Some roles can't switch off." True. Emergency clinicians, single parents, first-responders, and editors at crisis desks live in on-call realities. For them, sabbath design moves from *ban* to *buffer*. *Show*: an emergency department in Glasgow staggers micro-sabbaths—ten minutes device-quiet between clusters of cases; the consultant carries the crash bleep; others breathe. *Name*: micro-harbour. *Explain*: even slim, predictable buffers restore enough executive function to prevent escalation from creeping into every exchange. *Implication*: staff report fewer sharp words at shift end and fewer charting errors. Scale down the harbour. Keep the lights.

A further counterpoint: "Won't pausing harm responsiveness?" Not if you specify and publish exceptions. Perlow's teams documented escalation trees; France's firms negotiated sector-specific carve-outs; hospitals post bleeps and bleep-holders. The art is not to wish emergencies away but to route them cleanly. When everyone knows the emergency lane, ordinary traffic calms; people stop treating all messages as fire engines. Responsiveness improves because it is reserved for real fires.

We should also guard against moral theatre. A company can declare sabbaths while quietly rewarding weekend heroics; a family can pin a contract and break it nightly. People notice the gap and stop believing. The remedy is alignment: defaults and sabbaths must reinforce each other. Scheduled send should be on; phones should wake in silent mode; calendars should show seams. A sabbath surrounded by noise is decorative. A sabbath supported by defaults is structural.

Iteration is what saves this from sanctimony. Treat sabbaths as prototypes. Write the purpose in a sentence; run a fortnight pilot; hold a five-minute review; adjust; try again for three weeks; publish the small wins. Perlow's success at BCG rested less on charisma than on repetition and measurement (Perlow, 2012). Sonnentag's work suggests the same: detachment strengthens with routines people understand and own (Sonnentag, 2012). The harbour gets better with tides.

One last image of the harbour, then the practical test. It is dusk. The studio light dims. The auto-reply wakes. The on-call list sits visible. A short chime sounds. Some people leave for trains; some read; one finishes a paragraph with a pencil. Messages queue like small boats outside the mouth of the bay. They will enter in the morning, one by one, when the tide is right. Work does not vanish. It aligns.

The unresolved question is deliberately sharp: *What is the narrowest, most truthful purpose for a sabbath you could keep for the next month without lying to your life?* Name that purpose—reactive-free, creative-only, family-first, repair-bound. Hang a light at the harbour mouth: a chime, a lamp, an auto-reply that states the lane for emergencies. Review after two weeks. If reactivity drops and rework falls, keep the walls. If not, move the stones. Rest is a practice. Make it compatible with the work you love by giving it a place to return to.

Chapter 7
Work Without Whiplash

In February 2018, engineers at a global software firm tracked a simple number: task switches per hour. The average was seventeen. Every few minutes, a developer dropped one context, opened another, then another—Slack ping, Jira ticket, meeting link, inbox, back to code. Productivity dashboards glowed green, yet real progress thinned. After three months of measurement and experiment, the team made a radical change: fewer meetings, structured handovers, and two uninterrupted "single-thread" days per week. The number fell to five. Quality scores rose by 23 per cent. Staff stopped joking about "attention whiplash." The relief was measurable, not sentimental.

The experiment's lesson was elegant and brutal. The modern workplace does not merely waste time; it fractures attention so often that no hour remains whole. Tools designed to connect us have dissolved the natural seams of work into a slurry of perpetual partial focus. We are constantly reacting, rarely completing. Most teams now live in what cognitive psychologists call *continuous partial attention*, a state of vigilance that mimics productivity but quietly burns it. What this chapter argues—what you will learn to design—is how to build work patterns that repair that fracture without romanticising slowness. The goal is not leisure. It is lucidity.

Work Without Whiplash asks a simple, exacting question: how can we sustain velocity without losing coherence? How do we move fast without disintegrating into fragments? The answer, this chapter will show, lies in architecture, not heroics—in systems that restore rhythm, protect depth, and treat time as a shared, moral asset rather than a private battleground. The antidote to whiplash is not willpower; it is design.

The first design principle is *single-threading*. The human brain is poor at parallelism; every switch costs energy, time, and memory consolidation. Yet the myth of multitasking remains our most persistent corporate superstition. We glorify the person with twenty tabs open as if attention were an assembly line. Neuroscientific studies since the early 2000s (Rubinstein, Meyer & Evans, 2001) show switching tasks can cut effective output by up to 40 per cent. The issue is not competence; it is cognitive tax. When we learn to structure days around single threads—discrete blocks of deep work with clear handovers—we reclaim both attention and dignity. Templates for such design exist in the kanban systems of Toyota (1953), where each worker owned one visible flow and a standardised handover. The principle was industrial. Its effect was human: one task, finished well.

But attention management cannot stop at the individual. A worker's rhythm is only as steady as their meeting calendar allows. Meetings are the centrifuge where attention fragments fastest. Each invite is a small tax on clarity, often disguised as collaboration. The problem is rarely malevolence; it is design drift. Meetings multiply because they are the default response to uncertainty. This chapter will show how to treat them instead as contracts for attention: every session with a defined purpose, a reading prime beforehand, and a closing reflection after. When meetings regain ritual structure—opening breath, explicit attention roles, a few minutes of silence for synthesis—they become less like interruptions and more like instruments. Time regains its shape.

Evidence bears this out. A 2022 study by Microsoft's Human Factors Lab used EEG monitoring to show that back-to-back meetings without breaks cause cumulative stress spikes, while even a five-minute pause resets brainwave patterns towards calm. The implication is moral as much as neurological: the cost of unstructured collaboration is carried by the nervous system. A calendar is a health document as well as a productivity one. Designing "meeting SLAs"—service level agreements for how we spend collective time—might sound corporate, but in practice it reclaims humanity. The SLA says: *we respect your focus; we end on time; we pause before the next storm.*

The same ethics must reach our digital correspondence. Email, once a marvel of asynchronous grace, has decayed into a ceaseless chat stream. The inbox that was meant to free us from the tyranny of the phone now demands perpetual vigilance. The historical irony is striking. When Ray Tomlinson sent the first email in 1971, the novelty was not speed but *distance*. It was correspondence—a letter that travelled quietly through code. To restore email's dignity, we must treat it again as correspondence, not conversation. A well-crafted message is not an instant exchange but an act of clarity. Three sentences. A subject line that states intent. Links in an appendix, not a scroll of prose. Brevity, not brusqueness.

This reframing is not nostalgia. It is operational hygiene. Teams that adopt slower, clearer correspondence reduce escalation loops and rework. In 2020, Basecamp's internal audit of communications showed that restricting email and chat to time-bound windows cut misinterpretations by half. Likewise, when Shopify declared a "calendar purge" and "meeting reset" in January 2023, it simultaneously reduced internal chat channels by 30 per cent, explicitly tying message volume to decision latency. These were not wellness gestures. They were efficiency reforms grounded in cognitive ergonomics.

Urgency—our final theme—demands the same re-architecture. Many workplaces have mistaken constant availability for care, confusing *speed of response* with *quality of resolution*. True urgency is rare. Most crises are design failures in disguise. To distinguish the two, teams need *incident playbooks* and *escalation trees*, not perpetual vigilance. Borrowing from the aviation principle of "blast-radius thinking"—limiting how many people a problem can disrupt—some software firms now define what constitutes a genuine emergency in writing. Pager rotations in healthcare and DevOps exist for the same reason: to protect the non-on-call majority from pseudo-urgency. Calm is not the absence of pressure; it is pressure with boundaries.

Work without whiplash, then, is neither pastoral fantasy nor productivity fetish. It is an applied ethic: designing environments that match the limits and strengths of human attention. The philosophy behind it is ancient—Marcus Aurelius writing his *Meditations* before dawn, monks in Cluny ringing bells to shape the day, artisans in Edo Japan practising *shokunin kishitsu* (craftsmanship spirit) through ordered repetition. Each culture discovered that rhythm dignifies effort. The tools have changed. The principle has not.

To work sanely now is to remember that speed and serenity are not opposites but partners in tension. Systems that honour both produce fewer errors, less burnout, and more beauty in output. This chapter will show how to craft such systems—through single-threaded calendars, attentive meetings, humane correspondence, and bounded urgency. Each section is practical and philosophical in equal measure: templates that you can test, but also lenses that can reframe what you call work itself.

You will leave with more than time-management tricks. You will leave with a deeper grammar for focus—one that allows modern work to be both fast and faithful to thought. The payoff is collective, not private: organisations that move without whiplash make better decisions, waste less intelligence, and return home on time with their minds intact.

The question that follows, and that this chapter will help you answer, is deceptively simple: *If attention is the currency of modern work, how much of yours is spent on purpose—and how much is simply leaked?* The chapters ahead will not ask you to slow down. They will ask you to move differently, so that speed no longer tears at meaning.

Single-Thread Days

In March 2021, the design team at Atlassian's Sydney office ran a two-month experiment they called *Focus Fridays*. All meetings were banned from noon onwards; Slack notifications were muted by default. The company's internal telemetry, tracking commits, design prototypes, and ticket resolution, showed a 23 per cent increase in completed "deep tasks" during those half-days compared to multi-meeting Fridays. Quality scores from peer review also rose. What startled managers most was not the productivity spike but the mood shift—employees reported finishing the week "clear-headed" rather than "drained." The change had less to do with hours gained than with *threads restored.*

The modern calendar is a centrifuge. Emails, calls, pings, dashboards—each tugs our attention into fragments. We spend days that look full but feel hollow, packed with partial efforts that never cohere. The problem is not work itself but the way we slice it. Research from the American Psychological Association (Rubinstein, Meyer & Evans, 2001) estimated that task switching can consume up to 40 per cent of productive time. More recent field studies by Gloria Mark at the University of California, Irvine, found the average worker changes digital contexts every 47 seconds (Mark, 2022). Each switch triggers a micro-cost: re-orienting memory, reconstructing context, resetting emotion. The total is a silent tax on depth.

Single-thread days reclaim that depth by design. *Show*: one engineer codes for four hours, phone silenced, calendar blocked. *Name*: single-thread day. *Explain*: a period devoted to one cognitively demanding sequence—writing, designing, analysing, or deciding—bookended by clear handovers to the next domain. *Implication*: fewer errors, faster ramp-up, steadier morale. The brain's attentional networks prefer rhythm to chaos; sustained focus is metabolically efficient once entered. Switching, by contrast, burns glucose and goodwill alike.

The motif here is the *lane*. Multitasking promises a motorway of progress but delivers a car park of collisions. A lane, by contrast, offers friction and flow together. To single-thread is to choose a lane and stay there long enough to arrive somewhere worth reaching.

Kanban boards, first formalised at Toyota in 1953, remain the purest expression of this principle. Each card moves visibly through states—To Do, Doing, Done—so that attention aligns with progress rather than chaos. When Toyota's engineers introduced *Andon* cords, allowing any worker to pause the line and focus on fixing a fault, they institutionalised deep work inside an industrial rhythm. The practice has since migrated into software development and research planning. Atlassian, Asana, and Trello (ironically, a company Atlassian later acquired) all encode this lineage: constrain visible work, limit work in progress, finish before starting anew. The outcome is not rigidity but flow with feedback.

Consider a contrasting example: an academic department with 12 simultaneous grant proposals, each requiring partial attention from the same three administrators. Every week, new urgencies interrupt old ones. Deadlines blur; quality falls; weekends disappear. A study of UK university administrators (Research England, 2020) found that average "context fragments" per day exceeded 70—emails, calls, spreadsheet updates, each demanding re-entry into a different mental file. When the team adopted a visual Kanban and dedicated Tuesdays to a single grant family, output rose while overtime halved. The design principle was not moral restraint but queue discipline.

Checklists, too, underpin single-thread work. When Atul Gawande and the World Health Organization introduced the Surgical Safety Checklist in 2008, complications fell by over a third (Haynes et al., *NEJM*, 2009). The checklist's genius was not bureaucracy but bandwidth: it externalised memory, freeing attention for precision. In creative or analytical work, a pre-flight list—documents ready, goals defined, context reviewed—plays the same role. It drains anxiety before focus begins. Harvard Business School's Teresa Amabile has shown that even brief planning rituals increase "perceived progress" and intrinsic motivation (Amabile & Kramer, 2011). The mind relaxes when the lane ahead is lit.

Single-thread design also depends on *handover*. Without explicit transition, focus collapses into guilt about what's next. The most effective teams write short *handover notes* at the close of each block: what was done, what remains, what's blocked, what's next. This mirrors aviation's flight-deck briefings, where clear verbal transitions reduce cognitive residue between shifts. A day that ends with a written handover can begin tomorrow without friction.

Two more named, checkable cases make the pattern visible. At *Microsoft Japan* in August 2019, the company tested a four-day week with strict single-thread work blocks. Meetings were capped at 30 minutes, emails discouraged during deep-work hours, and teams were required to hand over tasks visibly in shared boards. Productivity, measured as sales per employee, rose by 40 per cent (Microsoft Japan, 2019). In the Netherlands, *The Behavioural Insights Team* partnered with Utrecht University in 2021 to test "focus sprints"—two-hour, no-notification blocks twice weekly. Participants reported 65 per cent fewer self-interruptions and a measurable improvement in decision accuracy on complex policy briefs. Across sectors, when lanes tighten, clarity expands.

The counter-example is seductive: creative serendipity often arises from cross-pollination. Multi-threaded work, some argue, fuels innovation by exposing the mind to diverse inputs. It's a fair claim—but misread. The problem is not diversity of stimuli but simultaneity. Creative breakthroughs occur when different threads have time to integrate in background cognition, a process neuroscientists call *incubation*. Constant switching starves incubation by never letting any thread settle. The reconciliation is rhythmic variety, not chaos: one lane at a time, but multiple lanes across a week.

Calendars reveal belief systems. A reactive calendar fragments thought into micro-units; a designed calendar protects coherence. *Show*: a researcher divides the week into three deep-work days and two interaction days. *Name*: single-thread template. *Explain*: depth receives space proportional to its cognitive weight, and meetings cluster into seams between blocks. *Implication*: each day retains an identifiable shape. In high-noise environments—consulting, medicine, education—even half-days suffice. The visible pattern signals permission to colleagues: this time has a purpose; interruption costs.

Templates help operationalise ideals. The "Focus-Collab-Admin" model used at several European design studios assigns a single dominant thread per day: focus (creation), collaboration (meetings), administration (updates). The rotation prevents backlog while giving each domain its full metabolic rhythm. A more granular variant—the "2-3-1" schedule—allocates two hours deep work in the morning, three hours interaction mid-day, one hour review before close. Both borrow from research on circadian attention peaks (Schmidt et al., *PNAS*, 2007): deep focus aligns best with late-morning alpha rhythms, while afternoons tolerate lighter switching. The science matters only because it confirms what craft already knew: concentration has climate zones.

Metrics make the invisible visible. Track interruptions per hour, context switches per day, and completed deep-work sessions per week. When these numbers improve, fatigue falls faster than volume. In Atlassian's *Focus Fridays*, average Slack messages per person dropped from 270 to 180 without reducing collaboration output.

Cognitive bandwidth behaves like a scarce resource; when rationed wisely, it compounds.

The motif of the *lane* returns in a moral light. A lane is not a cage but a covenant: it says *I will give this attention my best, and I trust you to guard it while I do.* Teams that protect each other's lanes generate mutual calm, a collective rhythm stronger than any policy. Psychologist Mihály Csíkszentmihályi's research on flow found that the state depends less on individual traits than on environment—clear goals, immediate feedback, reduced distraction. Single-thread days institutionalise those conditions. Flow becomes normal, not mystical.

Limitations persist. Some work, especially operational or client-facing, resists neat single-threading. Emergencies erupt; dependencies collide. Yet even here, principles scale. Clear *handover rituals*—a two-minute verbal brief, a visible board update, or an end-of-day note—anchor fragments into continuity. One NHS digital transformation team in Leeds adopted 90-minute "no-switch zones" during a pandemic surge in 2020. They could not choose silence, but they could choose seams. Even 90 minutes, repeated, reshaped fatigue patterns. The brain recognised a lane, however short.

The cultural shift required is subtle: from celebrating responsiveness to valuing *responsible focus*. Many teams prize instant replies as proof of engagement, but this norm corrodes craftsmanship. A delayed but thoughtful response, framed by single-thread work, often produces better outcomes and lower stress. Cal Newport's research on "deep work" (2016) and computer-science studies on software defect rates converge here: sustained attention improves quality exponentially. Whiplash speed kills the very velocity it seeks.

Designing for single-thread days demands courage because it makes commitments visible. Declaring a lane means saying *no* to false urgencies. It also redistributes status: the loudest person no longer wins the hour. When deep work becomes public and protected, hierarchy flattens around competence. The implications for leadership are profound. To protect focus is to protect trust.

The unresolved tension is this: can organisations built on acceleration accept deliberate rhythm without mistaking it for slowness? The forward test is behavioural, not rhetorical. Audit your next week. Count the switches. How many true lanes exist? Then choose one day to protect a single thread—end to end, with handover notes and visible seams. If your quality rises and fatigue falls, the experiment has already proved its case. The lane is open.

Meetings That Respect Attention

In March 2022, Shopify's chief operating officer, Kaz Nejatian, deleted 12,000 recurring meetings from employee calendars in a single morning. The act was not impulsive. Shopify's analytics team had tracked meeting volume, length, and attendance over three months and discovered that a typical manager spent 18 hours a week in meetings—more than double their focused work time. Productivity surveys showed declining morale and "meeting fatigue" scores rising by 27 per cent. After the purge, the company introduced explicit *meeting SLAs*—service-level agreements defining purpose, participants, and frequency—and required all new recurring meetings to be justified afresh. Within six weeks, internal telemetry revealed a measurable reduction in meeting hours, but decision throughput—tracked through completed projects—actually increased. Less conversation, more conclusion.

The paradox was ancient but newly visible: collaboration thrives not on contact but on *clarity*. The human brain, evolved for serial focus, struggles when too many voices, screens, and decisions collide in real time. The average meeting, according to data from Microsoft's Human Factors Lab (2021), now lasts 41 minutes and involves at least nine participants. Brainwave monitoring shows cumulative stress spikes between sessions with no breaks. Each unstructured conversation becomes an attentional debt, carried forward into the next task. When attention erodes, so does collective intelligence.

To repair this, we must treat meetings not as standing rituals but as *designed attention events*—temporary gatherings built around purpose, rhythm, and recovery. The motif throughout this chapter is the *circle*: a space intentionally bounded so that focus can hold. The best circles—monastic councils, jazz quartets, design sprints—share a grammar: defined entry, shared tempo, and clean exit. Meetings that respect attention revive that grammar for knowledge work.

Show: a 30-minute product review opens with a one-page reading prime, participants silent for the first five minutes, screens off except for the document. *Name*: Amazon's "narrative memo" method, formalised by Jeff Bezos in 2004. *Explain*: written memos replace slides, forcing structured thinking before speech; the silent reading period ensures everyone begins from the same cognitive ground. *Implication*: decisions accelerate because attention synchronises. Empirical studies of written-briefing formats (Kirkpatrick, Harvard Business Review, 2021) show higher decision satisfaction and lower follow-up load. Silence, paradoxically, saves time.

At Bridgewater Associates, the world's largest hedge fund, every meeting since 2015 has included an *attention role*—a participant explicitly responsible for monitoring conversational drift. The role rotates weekly and carries social authority to call "pause" when dialogue slides into noise. The behavioural economist Iris Bohnet at Harvard Kennedy School has shown that assigning metacognitive roles—timekeeper, summariser, or challenger—reduces "shared information bias", the tendency for groups to revisit what they already know. A meeting gains intelligence when someone protects its perimeter.

The second design principle is the *end-cap*. Most meetings dissipate without closure, leaving cognitive residue. At IDEO's London studio, facilitators introduced two-minute reflection rounds after workshops: each participant speaks one insight or decision aloud before leaving. The act fixes memory and exposes drift. Neuropsychological research by Mueller and Oppenheimer (2014) demonstrates that verbal synthesis consolidates recall more effectively than passive review. The end-cap is not sentiment; it is scaffolding. It translates talk into trace.

A visible meeting SLA crystallises these ethics. Shopify's post-purge model required that every meeting invite contain five fields: Purpose (why gather?), Product (what deliverable?), People (who truly needed?), Periodicity (how often?), and Pause (what default rest?). These fields worked as small contracts for attention. The moral shift was subtle but real: time became a shared asset rather than private property. When every participant's hour carries equal weight, the calculus of invitation changes.

Compare this with the pathology of "open invite" culture. In one Fortune 500 technology firm (anonymous, internal audit 2020), 38 per cent of meeting attendees contributed nothing verbally, yet their collective cost—measured by average hourly rate—exceeded £22 million annually. The audit spurred a radical experiment: meetings above five participants required pre-circulated reading primes and explicit decision metrics. Within four months, meeting time dropped by 35 per cent, and project delivery rates improved by 14 per cent. The firm learned that the true cost of a bad meeting is not boredom—it is compound distraction.

Counter-examples reveal nuance. Pixar's famed "Braintrust" sessions, where directors and storytellers gather to critique films in progress, are long, messy, and emotionally charged. They lack strict agendas by design. Creativity demands some friction and ambiguity. Yet even there, rules of attention persist: phones banned, laptops closed, notes handwritten. The circle holds because it is bounded by trust and ritual. Pixar's method demonstrates that respecting attention does not mean sterilising it. Freedom thrives within form.

To generalise from these cases: attention-respectful meetings balance *preparation*, *presence*, and *pause*. Preparation includes reading primes—brief written contexts distributed in advance so participants arrive aligned. Presence means active listening, with roles that anchor awareness. Pause provides closure and reflection. When these three phases align, meeting ROI—measured as decisions per hour or follow-up tasks completed—rises sharply. A 2022 MIT Sloan study found that teams using pre-reads and reflection rounds made 30 per cent fewer revisiting decisions within two weeks. The brain, it turns out, forgets less when it finishes properly.

The image of the *circle* returns here as both structure and ethic. Ancient councils—from Athens' *ekklesia* to the Buddhist *sangha*—began with ritual stillness. Modern equivalents might start with 60 seconds of silence or a slow reading of the purpose statement. These gestures matter. Microsoft's experiments with "mindful meeting openings" during 2021–22 showed a measurable drop in EEG stress markers and improved post-meeting focus scores. The reason is not mystical. Shared silence equalises hierarchy; it grants everyone the same moment of arrival.

Practical design extends into metrics. Count meetings per week, average attendees, and follow-up volume. At a London-based NGO, after introducing meeting SLAs and attention roles in early 2023, total meeting hours fell 28 per cent, but project completion times improved. Surveys found the perceived quality of meetings—clarity, emotional tone, and fairness—rose by 40 per cent. Numbers measure what attention feels like when respected: lighter, sharper, and more just.

Technology can amplify or erode this ethic. Calendar software now allows enforced buffers between meetings; tools like Clockwise and Reclaim automatically protect focus zones. Yet these automations are only as humane as the norms behind them. A team that auto-schedules rest but punishes delay learns nothing. A meeting policy must pair digital restraint with social permission—to decline, to pause, to think. Without cultural endorsement, software becomes choreography without rhythm.

A case worth studying comes from the UK's *Government Digital Service* (GDS) in 2019. Facing coordination chaos across 14 departments, they restructured all cross-team meetings under "attention charters." Every session began with a two-minute reading prime, one facilitator, one scribe, and a reflection note published the same day. Within six months, reported meeting satisfaction rose 60 per cent, while meeting frequency dropped by a third. Civil servants who once described meetings as "draining" began calling them "coherent." The difference was not temperament but architecture.

Sceptics argue that such discipline risks sterility. Too many protocols, they say, suffocate spontaneity. The tension is real. Yet history suggests that form and freedom coexist. Jazz improvisation depends on agreed time signatures; parliamentary debate on standing orders. Attention flourishes when it knows its container. The question, therefore, is not how to loosen meetings but how to *tune* them—to their purpose, duration, and stakes.

The philosophy behind attention-respectful meetings is democratic at its core. Every participant's cognition is treated as valuable. To waste attention is to waste shared intelligence. When teams see time as common property, politeness becomes policy. The small ritual of asking, *"Do we need to meet?"* before sending an invite restores this ethic. The answer is often no—but when yes, it deserves full presence.

There is also a spiritual undertone, whether or not named as such. A good meeting, like a well-run choir rehearsal, leaves participants quieter, not louder. It clarifies thought. It generates stillness, not just output. In 2017, the mindfulness teacher Jon Kabat-Zinn was invited to the UK Parliament to open a cross-party meeting with three minutes of silence. Lawmakers later described the ensuing debate as "calmer, more lucid." Attention, when respected, civilises discourse.

The unresolved question is deceptively practical: if your calendar reflects your values, what do your meetings reveal about yours? Audit the next week. How many sessions begin in silence, with purpose visible? How many end with reflection or decision clarity? How many protect the circle rather than fracture it? The answers will tell you not just how you work—but what kind of attention your culture believes is worth keeping.

Email as Correspondence Again

In October 1971, Ray Tomlinson, a computer engineer working at Bolt Beranek and Newman in Cambridge, Massachusetts, sent the first electronic message between two ARPANET machines standing side by side. The content—likely the meaningless string "QWERTYUIOP"—was trivial. The act was not. It marked the birth of email: a private letter transmitted instantly across a digital corridor. Tomlinson later admitted he almost didn't announce it. "It wasn't something I considered earth-shattering," he said in a 2009 interview. Yet the architecture he built would come to dominate professional communication for half a century. The tragedy is not that email became ubiquitous, but that it forgot it was correspondence.

The average office worker now receives 121 emails and sends 40 daily (Radicati Group, 2023). What was once asynchronous and reflective has become relentless and reactive. The inbox—once the quiet desk of digital life—has turned into an arena of perpetual triage. Most messages are written in haste, read in fragments, and answered without thought. Cognitive scientists estimate that each inbox check, even brief, costs up to 64 seconds of reorientation (Mark et al., University of California, Irvine, 2014). Multiply that across a workday, and entire afternoons dissolve into the noise of partial communication. The problem is not technology; it is tempo.

To restore email's dignity, we must reclaim it as a medium of correspondence: slower, clearer, and fewer. That phrase—*email as correspondence*—is both principle and practice. It recognises that language gains power when it travels with intention, not urgency. The motif here is the *letter*: a form that demands thought before dispatch. Letters carried weight because they travelled slowly. That slowness made the sender precise. The digital letter can still hold that weight, if we re-engineer its grammar.

The first element of that grammar is the *subject-line contract.* Each message should declare its purpose in miniature: *Decision needed by Friday: Q3 budget sign-off*; *Info only: revised design mock-ups attached.* Such clarity pre-allocates attention. The reader knows whether to act, archive, or await context. This principle, now adopted by firms like Basecamp and Automattic, has quantifiable benefits. Basecamp's 2021 internal analysis showed a 37 per cent reduction in average reply chains after adopting explicit subject-line tagging. The act of naming purpose reduces interpretive friction. The subject line becomes a handshake: concise, courteous, and complete.

Next comes the *three-sentence body.* This constraint—pioneered in writing protocols at Stripe and the BBC's digital departments—forces clarity by compression. The first sentence states purpose. The second conveys context. The third signals next action or closure. Everything else lives in appendices or links. The rule is not aesthetic but neurological. Studies in cognitive load theory (Sweller, 1998) show that working memory peaks at three to four information chunks before comprehension falters. Email that respects that limit becomes readable again. At Stripe, adoption of the "three-sentence" discipline cut average internal email reading time by 22 per cent.

The appendices—hyperlinked, not pasted—complete the structure. They allow depth without clutter. A short note might link to a shared document or decision log, keeping the body as a map, not a landfill. This mirrors the footnote logic of scholarly writing: surface brevity, buried depth. The paradox is that slower writing speeds communication. When thought is front-loaded, reply chains shrink. As economist Herbert Simon observed in 1971, "a wealth of information creates a poverty of attention." The digital letter reverses that poverty through deliberate scarcity.

Two historical parallels illuminate the point. In the 18th century, letters between the British Royal Society's Fellows—Hooke, Boyle, Newton—often stretched to several pages yet followed strict conventions: salutation, hypothesis, result, reply. Each missive was both record and argument. The speed was glacial, but the discourse cumulative. Centuries later, when Vannevar Bush imagined the "memex" in 1945, his vision of linked documents prefigured email—but with an embedded ethic of reflection. Bush wrote of information "growing in trails," not streams. The correspondence metaphor shaped the very foundations of the digital age. Its loss is not nostalgia but amnesia.

Modern organisations that rediscover this ethic see tangible gains. At *GitLab*, the world's largest all-remote company, asynchronous communication is a corporate creed. Every employee handbook section begins with "Write, don't chat." Emails and memos serve as permanent records, written for clarity and future reference. Meetings are rare, messages crafted for precision. The result: a fully distributed workforce spanning more than sixty countries operates without constant chatter. Attention is preserved as a shared resource. Similarly, *Basecamp's* "Hey" email platform (launched 2020) reintroduces batching, explicit send-later defaults, and threadless correspondence to protect focus. Both firms prove that slow mail can power fast work.

The counter-example comes from chat-driven cultures where immediacy masquerades as efficiency. Slack, Microsoft Teams, and similar tools were built to streamline coordination, yet their design—real-time notifications, typing indicators, endless threads—encourages conversational entropy. The MIT Sloan School (2022) studied 20,000 workers across firms that adopted Slack. While message volume soared, meaningful collaboration dropped. Teams self-reported higher stress and shallower decisions. The convenience of constant reachability eroded the discipline of reflection. The medium collapsed into noise.

Reconciling these extremes requires not rejection but boundary design. Email as correspondence reclaims the middle ground: asynchronous, deliberate, and traceable. The calendar reinforces this rhythm. Many teams now schedule "correspondence windows"—hourly blocks for reading and writing mail, separate from deep work. The result mirrors the postal metaphor: delivery and reply have cadence. A 2023 internal pilot at Siemens UK tested fixed email windows (11:00 and 16:00). Inbox traffic remained stable, but response quality scores—rated by clarity and completeness—rose by 29 per cent. The constraint bred coherence.

The moral dimension is worth naming. To write a careful email is to grant the reader respect. It assumes their attention is finite and valuable. The act of editing before sending is an act of empathy. In contrast, to forward impulsively or type without pause is to treat another's cognition as disposable. The 18th-century essayist Lord Chesterfield called careless letters "an imposition on friendship." The same could be said of modern work relationships. The quality of a culture can be read in its inbox.

There are templates for dignity. The *Calm Company* movement, spearheaded by Jason Fried and David Heinemeier Hansson, codifies correspondence norms: no expectation of instant reply, explicit next steps, and courteous closure. The last is crucial. Emails that end with "Thank you for considering" or "No reply needed" restore asymmetry to time: the sender does not dictate the recipient's rhythm. This etiquette, when scaled, rebalances professional respect. A study by Harvard's Program on Negotiation (Curhan & Elfenbein, 2018) found that politeness in digital correspondence correlates strongly with trust and follow-through. Language sets the moral tone of collaboration.

There are limits, of course. Some communication demands speed—incident response, live coordination, care work. Yet even here, channels can specialise. Emergency teams use clear escalation paths; aviation uses "read-backs" for precision. Urgency and clarity are not enemies. The problem arises when every message claims crisis status. Email's strength is its resistance to that inflation. Its asynchronous nature is a feature, not a flaw.

The motif of the *letter* returns. A good letter lives longer than its sender's mood. It can be re-read, quoted, and understood across time zones and tempers. Email, when written as correspondence, acquires the same longevity. It becomes not a message but a micro-document, capable of guiding decisions weeks later. The inbox, redesigned around correspondence, becomes a collective memory rather than a battlefield.

Evidence from organisational psychology supports this. A 2020 study in *Computers in Human Behavior* found that asynchronous written communication improves "perceived autonomy" and "reduced emotional exhaustion." Workers who set clear response boundaries and wrote longer, more structured emails reported higher job satisfaction. The slower pace preserved agency. The implicit promise of email-as-correspondence is not just clarity but calm.

Yet adopting it requires courage. Fast replies have become social currency. To pause before responding feels rebellious. But rebellion, in this context, is leadership. A manager who models slower correspondence signals that thought outranks haste. A team that measures clarity instead of responsiveness changes its metabolism. Cultural transformation begins in the inbox.

The unresolved question lingers: can a medium built for speed sustain meaning through slowness? The answer depends on what we choose to value—immediacy or intelligence, throughput or thought. The next time you compose an email, test a simple rule: if this message were printed and delivered by hand, would it still deserve to exist? If not, perhaps it was never correspondence at all.

When Urgency Is Real

On 28 February 2017, in Northern Virginia, a mistyped command during a routine maintenance task took Amazon's S3 storage service offline in the US-EAST-1 region. The ripple effects were global. Thousands of sites and apps stalled; status pages buckled under load. Amazon's subsequent post-mortem detailed operator error, inadequate tooling safeguards, and a missing "blast-radius" constraint; it also outlined changes: partitioned control planes, slower-is-safer playbooks, and a firmer incident command structure (Amazon, 2017, US-EAST-1). The lesson landed far beyond cloud engineering: urgency without architecture multiplies harm. Urgency with architecture limits it. Urgency without design becomes noise.

Real crises compress time. They demand speed and judgement under conditions of partial information. Yet the modern workplace often treats *everything* as urgent. The physiological results are predictable: tunnel vision, brittle communication, needless escalation. The organisational results are worse: chronic pseudo-urgency that corrodes trust and degrades decisions. Distinguishing signal from noise is therefore not a soft skill. It is an operational ethic. This subchapter sets out the mechanics of that ethic: incident playbooks, escalation trees, on-call rotations, and the discipline of blast-radius thinking, so that calm survives contact with the problem.

Begin with the thing itself: the *incident. Show*: a payment service fails at 09:17; dashboards redden; customers cannot check out. *Name*: incident command. *Explain*: a pre-agreed role set—Incident Commander, Communications Lead, Subject-Matter Responders—activates with a single call-word; one person holds the radio and the timeline, others work the problem, a separate voice updates stakeholders. *Implication*: cognitive load divides; panic does not. Google's *Site Reliability Engineering* (Beyer et al., 2016) describes this pattern in detail, emphasising single-threaded command to avoid "chat-ops chaos." NHS England's *Emergency Preparedness, Resilience and Response* framework (EPRR; 2015, updated 2022) codifies a parallel structure for major incidents, with Bronze-Silver-Gold command tiers that stabilise decision flow under pressure. Forms differ; the principle holds: roles before rush.

Playbooks make roles executable. *Show*: a runbook titled "Payments: High Error Rates" hangs off the on-call pager; it lists first five checks, rollback commands, comms template, and escalation thresholds. *Name*: incident playbook. *Explain*: in a crisis, we outsource memory to text so that judgement can focus on *choice*, not *recall. Implication*: mean-time-to-acknowledge (MTTA) drops; mean-time-to-restore (MTTR) follows. Etsy's culture of blameless post-mortems (Allspaw, Velocity, 2012) emerged from this logic: write down what failed; update the playbook; remove shame so learning travels. When the text improves, the system improves.

Escalation trees prevent the most common failure of all: everyone, everywhere, "helping" at once. *Show*: "If X persists after Y minutes or exceeds Z customers, page Team A; if no response in 5 minutes, page Team B; if P1 sustained for 30 minutes, notify Legal and PR via template." *Name*: escalation tree. *Explain*: bounded routes replace megaphone channels; the loudest person no longer sets the tempo. *Implication*: blast-radius stays small; the majority continue useful work; only the on-call few absorb the noise. In healthcare this logic is old: trauma teams page specific roles in sequence so corridors do not flood. In software, PagerDuty and Opsgenie simply mechanise triage that hospitals learned by bitter experience.

Blast-radius thinking is the governing motif. *Show*: the S3 control plane once allowed a single command to remove too many servers too quickly; after the outage, Amazon partitioned and rate-limited destructive actions (Amazon, 2017). *Name*: blast-radius discipline. *Explain*: assume failure and design to *contain* it—partition services, slow dangerous commands, gate risky changes behind dual control, and test fallbacks. *Implication*: when your failure happens—and it will—the damage stays local. A system that cannot be broken in small pieces will eventually break in one large piece.

The boundary between urgent and noisy is behavioural, not rhetorical. *Show*: a CTO marks every message "URGENT" in a company Slack; the channel dissolves into flares. *Name*: pseudo-urgency. *Explain*: when the label expands, the category dies; response quality falls because no one trusts the word. *Implication*: the real urgent event, when it comes, arrives to a deaf room. By contrast, organisations that reserve urgency for defined conditions—P1 criteria stated in advance, with examples—see higher compliance when the bell rings. The word regains its power.

Preparation communicates respect. *Show*: prewritten comms snippets—"We are investigating a service interruption affecting checkout for a subset of users; updates every 15 minutes"—sit in a shared folder. *Name*: comms cadence. *Explain*: during an incident, uncertainty is certain; cadence is controllable. A reliable ticker (every 15 minutes public; every 5 minutes internal) keeps rumour from growing in the gaps. *Implication*: customers feel held; staff stay coordinated; leaders can think. In aviation, sterile cockpit rules and standard phraseology serve the same end: language that protects bandwidth.

Two named, checkable cases make the distinctions concrete. First, the FAA's nationwide ground stop on 11 January 2023 after a corrupted NOTAM database forced flight crews to operate without reliable safety notices. The decision was blunt, costly, and correct: when an information system that protects life loses integrity, the blast-radius includes every runway. Ground the planes; then restore. *Implication*: authority means owning the pause. Second, on 13 January 2018, the Hawaii Emergency Management Agency issued a false ballistic missile alert to mobile phones. The on-screen message read: "This is not a drill." Panic followed. Investigations later cited poor interface design, inadequate confirmation prompts, and unclear drills. *Implication*: urgency systems without guardrails create harm greater than delay. The remedy is layered: two-person confirmation, unambiguous UI, and rigorous exercises with safe sandboxes.

Counter-examples deserve honesty. Pixar's "all-hands" story sessions or newsroom war rooms during elections can look like permanent emergencies—messy, high-energy, many voices. Yet their stakes differ. Creativity thrives on friction; aircraft and payment systems do not. The reconciliation is *domain specificity*: reserve incident machinery for systems where safety, money, or trust is on the line. Elsewhere, design lighter norms. Do not militarise creativity; do not improvise safety.

The physiology of crisis matters. Under acute stress the sympathetic system narrows perception; people fumble passwords and mis-type commands. Playbooks therefore include *exhale lines* and *time-outs*: one slow breath every ten minutes; rotate the keyboard every thirty. This is not wellness theatre; it is error reduction. Microsoft's Human Factors Lab (2021) has shown that even short breaks between intense sessions flatten cumulative stress spikes. Calm is a tool. Put it in the kit.

On-call rotations are the humane spine of urgency. *Show*: a rota distributes night and weekend duty evenly; compensatory rest is codified; incident caps per responder are tracked. *Name*: sustainable on-call. *Explain*: vigilance is finite; beyond a point, humans hallucinate urgency in the ordinary and miss the real signal. *Implication*: protected rest is not perk but safety measure. Google SRE's error-budget policy anchors the same ethic at system scale: when reliability drops below the agreed bar, feature work pauses so stability can be restored; speed yields to safety until the budget recovers (Beyer et al., 2016).

Post-mortems close the loop. *Show*: 48 hours after resolution, the team meets to reconstruct the incident from logs and memory; no blame, crisp timelines, specific remediations with owners and dates. *Name*: blameless post-mortem. *Explain*: the goal is system learning, not personal confession. *Implication*: people surface near-misses; playbooks improve; leaders fund fixes because evidence is written. Etsy institutionalised this practice a decade ago and published its method widely (Allspaw, 2012). The effect is cultural as much as technical: fear declines; candour expands.

Metrics keep urgency honest. MTTA and MTTR are obvious; add *pages per responder per week* (to catch burnout), *false-positive rate* (to quantify noise), and *blast-radius score* (number of users or systems affected per incident class). A team that proudly reports falling MTTR while pages per responder soar is not healthier; it is bleeding. Numbers must be read together.

Language choices matter in the thick of it. The words "stop", "hold", "confirm", "repeat"—spoken calmly by a designated commander—anchor the room. NHS major-incident scripts do this by design: *Standby. Declared. Major incident stand-down.* Clarity over speed. Similarly, a well-designed Slack/Teams incident channel begins with a pinned header: *Channel purpose, current IC, severity level, last update time, next update due.* A naming convention like *#inc-payments-p1-2025-06-14* keeps logs queryable. These small constraints prevent the flood from erasing the map.

The motif of *firebreaks* returns. Forest managers cut lines that starve a blaze; incident managers cut lines that starve panic. Firebreaks take the form of separations: one person speaks to executives; another speaks to customers; only the commander pages new roles; changes freeze unless approved. When a situation worsens, widen the firebreaks—reduce participants, slow the rate of change, and raise the frequency of updates. When a situation improves, narrow them. The room learns to breathe with the fire, not to shout at it.

There are limits and trade-offs. Over-bureaucratised incident processes can add delay where seconds matter; understaffed rotations can turn playbooks into theatre. The remedy is practice. Run game-days. Inject faults. Drill the pager. Amazon, Google, and Netflix popularised "chaos engineering" precisely to test blast-radius assumptions before fate does. In public services, the Civil Contingencies Act (UK, 2004) hard-wires multi-agency exercises for the same reason. Drills are not performative if they change the text you reach for at 03:12.

Psychology closes the circle. Nothing protects calm more than a culture that believes calm is permitted. Leaders model this by *slowing the question*—"Say again. What do we know?"—and by accepting bounded downtime after high-heat events. When the pager rests, the person must rest. When the budget is blown, features stop. When reliability wobbles, dashboards win the argument with roadmaps. Such decisions are not costs; they are investments in future speed. Move slowly now to move quickly later.

Two final images stay useful when the room gets loud. First, the *radio check*: at the start of an incident channel, each role says "online"; the commander repeats back. Now there is a net. Second, the *clock*: updates at 15-minute beats, even if the only sentence is "No change, still investigating." Silence breeds rumours; cadence breeds confidence. Calm is an artefact of rhythm. Build it.

The unresolved test is specific. If an urgent page arrived this hour, which three sentences would your Incident Commander speak first, and where is the text they would read from? If your answer is improvisation, noise will win. If your answer is a playbook, an escalation tree, and a visible firebreak, urgency will mean what it says—and your team will keep its nerve when it matters.

Chapter 8
The Stillness Protocol

In 1968, a NASA engineer named Jack Kinzler designed a small, deceptively simple device: a foldable tool that allowed Apollo astronauts to anchor their experiments on the moon's surface. It was called the *universal handling fixture*, though the crew nicknamed it "the bicycle handle." Elegant, compact, functional — it turned chaos into choreography. Every Apollo mission that followed used it. What Kinzler created wasn't just a tool; it was a ritual of order in an environment defined by uncertainty. The Stillness Protocol aims for the same effect — a human handling fixture for the noise of digital life.

Stillness, in this book, has never meant withdrawal. It is precision, not passivity — an act of design rather than drift. Yet knowing that is not the same as *doing* it. Readers reach this point having glimpsed attention reclaimed, practices rebalanced, urgency tamed. The question now shifts from theory to architecture: *How does one build a life that protects what has been learned?* This chapter answers by turning reflection into structure, philosophy into cadence, and intention into something measurable, renewable, and shared.

The Stillness Protocol begins with a pattern of four arrows: **Attention → Intention → Design → Practice.** Each arrow transforms reflection into movement. Attention observes; Intention names; Design rearranges; Practice sustains. The model looks clean because it has been tested — in creative studios, clinical psychology programmes, even in military training, where rituals of focus and decompression have long been paired. The pattern endures because it scales. It fits both the monk's routine and the manager's calendar. It is less a system than a cycle — one that resets the nervous system of modern work.

But systems fail when they start from denial. Most people claim to be overwhelmed yet cannot describe *by what.* So the first act of stillness is not escape but *diagnosis*. The protocol begins with a digital audit: the apps you open, the hours they claim, the emotions they produce, the losses they conceal. It does not judge. It measures. The difference is moral. Diagnosis is compassion armed with clarity; denial is ignorance disguised as control. The chapter will show how to replace abstraction with evidence — how to track attention leaks, log their triggers, and see your own data not as guilt, but as guidance.

From diagnosis follows intervention. The Stillness Protocol borrows from behavioural science: make change visible, limit scope, measure gain. It offers a ranked menu — interventions scored by effort and impact — and invites the reader to choose just three, commit for two weeks, and measure against their own value metrics: sleep, mood, focus, quality of presence. Small, sustained changes compound faster than grand intentions. This is how calm becomes cumulative.

The next move is the *charter* — a personal constitution of attention. Every serious craft has one: pilots have checklists, athletes have training plans, monks have vows. A stillness charter turns the same principle inward. It defines what deserves your bandwidth, what doesn't, and who holds you accountable. This is not a self-help diary; it is a contract with one's own cognition. It matures through revision. Once a month, you meet the document you wrote and ask, "Is this still true?" The act of amendment keeps stillness alive. Complacency kills practice; curiosity sustains it.

Throughout this chapter, stillness will be treated as a *discipline of renewal.* The Protocol is not a one-time detox but a rhythm: weekly audits, fortnightly interventions, monthly reflection. The analogy is biological — a metabolic cycle for the mind. Systems thinkers call it "homeostatic adaptation": the ability of a living system to recover equilibrium after stress. The difference between a mindful professional and a burned-out one is not effort, but recovery rate. Stillness is the recovery protocol.

The broader philosophy aligns with older wisdom. The Stoics practised *premeditatio malorum* — visualising disruption so they could meet it calmly. Buddhist monastics recited daily vows to recall intention before action. The Stillness Protocol translates those rituals into modern design language: calendars, dashboards, peer accountability, iteration. It closes the gap between ancient insight and digital behaviour, turning soft virtue into hard architecture.

The motif of *cadence* runs through every section. Rhythm is the secret of resilience. Athletes periodise training; musicians rest between notes; software teams sprint, pause, and retrospect. A life without rhythm is a life without repair. This chapter shows how to build a rhythm of thought — a sequence of stillnesses embedded in ordinary time. Attention becomes intention when rehearsed; intention becomes design when applied; design becomes practice when sustained.

We will also confront the fragility of maintenance. Every protocol eventually meets resistance: fatigue, distraction, relapse. The purpose of a charter is not to guarantee perfection, but to provide *return points* — coordinates for recalibration. You don't fail the Stillness Protocol by breaking it; you fail it by refusing to begin again. What matters is re-entry, not permanence. As in breathwork, exhale follows inhale; the point is not holding still, but returning there.

By the final section, stillness will no longer mean still. It will mean *stable under motion.* The professional who can pause without freezing, act without frenzy, and measure without mania is practising digital dharma in its mature form. The Stillness Protocol is how that composure becomes culture — first individually, then collectively.

And so the question shifts from "How do I escape the noise?" to "How do I design a life that stays clear even when the noise returns?" The answer, as you'll soon see, lies not in another app, but in an audit, a charter, a cadence — and the quiet courage to keep them alive.

Attention → Intention → Design → Practice

In December 2015, the operations team at Toyota's Motomachi plant introduced a curious experiment. Instead of tightening production schedules, they began scheduling *pauses*: structured two-minute intervals every hour for line workers to step back, breathe, and note what they were actually noticing. The idea came from Taiichi Ohno's original *andon cord* philosophy—stop the line to see clearly. Within a quarter, quality defects fell by 28 per cent, yet output did not decline. The intervention was not technological; it was attentional. The team had built a rhythm where awareness preceded action. The Stillness Protocol begins at the same hinge. Before any redesign of habit or system, attention must stabilise. From there, intention clarifies, design reorganises, and practice sustains.

The sequence—**Attention → Intention → Design → Practice**—forms the living grammar of stillness. Each arrow converts reflection into motion without losing precision. Attention is observation without interference. Intention gives that observation a vector. Design makes the vector visible in space and time. Practice tests it in lived reality. When rehearsed weekly, the cycle becomes not a technique but a metabolism—an operational way of being. Like Toyota's attention pauses, it treats awareness as infrastructure.

Attention is the diagnostic stage: seeing clearly before acting. Neuroscientist Amishi Jha's research with the US Army (Jha et al., *PNAS*, 2010) found that focused-attention training improved working memory and reduced mind-wandering under stress. In both military and corporate settings, attention audits perform the same function: measuring what captures energy before trying to reallocate it. In professional contexts, this means tracking not time but *quality of focus*: when during the day clarity peaks, which notifications fracture it, which environments restore it. Attention logs—the modern equivalent of Ohno's line diary—turn vague fatigue into data. Once visible, attention can be governed.

Yet attention without **intention** is surveillance of the self, not stewardship. Intention transforms noticing into aim. It answers a simple question: *For what purpose do I attend?* The philosopher Simone Weil wrote in 1942 that "attention is the rarest and purest form of generosity." She meant that true attention is never neutral—it is a gift directed toward something chosen. In organisational life, intention statements function as compact declarations of this choice. They are short, measurable, and moral: "I intend to write code that reduces user friction"; "I intend to mentor, not manage, this quarter." Such statements anchor agency where distraction would otherwise decide.

The next arrow, **Design**, gives form to those intentions. This is where philosophy meets scheduling. Design turns abstract desire into environmental cue. Architect Louis Kahn used to say that "a room is not a room without natural light." Behavioural scientists would add: a routine is not a routine without structure. Design changes can be minute—placing a phone outside the bedroom, setting two meeting-free mornings, colour-coding cognitive load zones in the calendar. These are not aesthetic tweaks but attentional scaffolds. The design principle here mirrors ergonomics: make the desired behaviour the path of least resistance.

Design also includes social architecture. The company *Doist*—maker of the productivity app *Todoist*—redesigned its internal communication rules in 2021 around asynchronous respect: no mandatory replies within 24 hours, all project updates templated for clarity. The result was paradoxical: fewer messages, richer collaboration. *Show* → *Name* → *Explain* → *Implication*: their redesign conserved attention and increased creative throughput. A well-designed system does not demand vigilance; it distributes it.

From design we cross to **Practice**—the arrow where theory earns its endurance. Practice translates one-off improvements into rhythm. In cognitive behavioural therapy, repetition consolidates change through "behavioural activation": acting into new states until the brain normalises them. In the Stillness Protocol, practice follows the same neuroplastic logic. Weekly rehearsals—reflection blocks, re-grounding walks, brief audits—turn isolated calm into an expected part of the week. The measure of maturity is not intensity but recurrence.

The cycle repeats: attention refreshed, intention renewed, design adjusted, practice reinforced. Each pass refines the system. Over time, it resembles a feedback loop more than a checklist. The motif of the *arrow* becomes literal—forward, adaptive, continuous. Google's *Re:Work* initiative (2018) used similar iterative cycles to improve team focus. They embedded weekly "pulse" reflections into project schedules, asking three questions: What drained attention? What supported it? What deserves redesign? Within two months, meeting loads dropped 15 per cent, and peer-rated productivity rose by 20 per cent. Systems that build reflection into the workflow require less rescue later.

Counter-example clarifies the need. Consider the "deep work" movements of the late 2010s. Many organisations tried to replicate Cal Newport's model of long focus blocks without adjusting team coordination norms. Employees faced fewer meetings but more asynchronous messages. Context-switching simply moved channels. The limitation wasn't intent but design coherence. Attention was trained, intention stated, yet the ecosystem contradicted both. The Stillness Protocol reconciles this by treating attention as systemic property, not personal virtue. You cannot practise stillness in a culture that rewards panic.

Measurement gives the sequence its backbone. In attention audits, the key metric is *interruption density*—the number of attention shifts per hour. In intention tracking, it becomes *alignment ratio*: how many daily actions advance declared aims. In design, it is *friction delta*: how many steps were removed between intention and execution. In practice, it is *cadence adherence*: how many cycles were completed as planned. None of these metrics exist to shame; they exist to translate self-perception into evidence. A protocol measured is a protocol that survives.

The deeper implication is philosophical. Each arrow corresponds to a different mode of knowing: *Attention* is empirical, *Intention* is ethical, *Design* is architectural, *Practice* is existential. Together, they form a bridge between cognition and conduct. This bridge prevents two common collapses: moral exhaustion without structure, and efficiency without meaning. The first leads to burnout masked as purpose; the second to precision without soul. The sequence balances both—clarity in motion, conscience in design.

Weekly rehearsal is the living proof of the model. A two-hour reflection slot—Friday afternoon, Sunday evening, Monday dawn—becomes the ritual hinge of the week. The steps are modest: scan attention logs, rewrite one intention statement, adjust one design constraint, renew one daily practice. The rhythm matters more than the scale. Rehearsal turns philosophy into cadence, much as a musician turns theory into muscle memory. The aim is fluency: stillness that no longer needs deliberate invocation.

The motif of *return* threads through the protocol. Each week is a circuit returning to itself. Attention fades, intention drifts, design decays, practice stiffens—and yet, by cycling back, clarity re-emerges. The pattern echoes biological rhythms: heartbeats, circadian cycles, breath. This is not metaphor but embodiment. Human systems, like natural ones, self-correct through periodic pause. Stillness is not a state to hold but a rhythm to renew.

Sceptics might object that life rarely allows such choreography—that emergencies, children, clients, and calendars dissolve protocols. True. Yet the cycle's resilience lies in its scale invariance: even ten minutes of honest attention can reset intention; a single design tweak can free an hour. The structure shrinks to fit the day available. The question is not *how much* time one has, but *how often* one remembers to begin.

The four arrows thus describe both process and promise: a framework that can be run like software or lived like ritual. Its power comes from its simplicity, its humility from iteration. As systems thinker Donella Meadows wrote, "We can't control systems, but we can dance with them." The Stillness Protocol is that dance: four steps, endlessly repeated, quietly refining a life that no longer confuses movement with progress.

The tension remains: can such cadence survive contact with the accelerating world? The test is not whether the world slows down, but whether the practitioner learns to pace within it—to build the line pauses that let vision return. The next arrow always begins where the last one ended: with attention, again.

Diagnose, Don't Deny

In February 2019, the design team at *Hootsuite*, the social media management company based in Vancouver, conducted a blunt internal audit. Employees were asked to log every platform they opened during a working day and record each session's start and end time. The result was sobering: an average of 137 platform switches per employee, per day. Designers found themselves toggling between analytics dashboards, Slack threads, email clients, and prototype tools so frequently that no one could recall how long they had actually *designed.* The team's director called it "a nervous system collapse by a thousand tabs." The audit didn't shame anyone. It did something better—it gave the problem boundaries. Once visible, the noise could be managed. This is the essence of diagnosis: making dysfunction explicit so that clarity becomes possible.

Denial, by contrast, is the art of staying busy while staying blind. It thrives in professionals who confuse awareness with control. "I'm fine," they say, while their sleep shortens, tabs multiply, and attention fractures. The Stillness Protocol begins where denial ends—with diagnosis that is calm, forensic, and kind. It teaches how to *see* digital life before judging it, because improvement without truth is theatre. Diagnosis is not a confession; it is a map.

Every effective protocol begins with inventory. *Show → Name → Explain → Implication. Show:* you spend 4.5 hours daily on your phone, according to your device's screen-time report. *Name:* two hours are in messaging apps, one in email, one in news feeds. *Explain:* that's 20 per cent of waking life filtered through glass. *Implication:* you do not need more discipline; you need better data. The audit makes denial impossible without invoking guilt. It replaces moralism with measurement.

A rigorous diagnosis has three layers: *apps*, *hours*, and *outcomes*. The first layer tracks exposure—what tools or platforms claim attention. The second measures investment—how much time and energy each absorbs. The third identifies effect—what each yields in value, harm, or neutrality. This three-tier approach mirrors the structure of cognitive-behavioural assessment: record stimulus, measure response, evaluate consequence. Applied digitally, it exposes hidden asymmetries. The apps that feel productive often erode focus; the ones that feel indulgent sometimes restore it. Without evidence, intuition lies.

Researchers at the University of Pennsylvania (Hunt et al., *Journal of Social and Clinical Psychology*, 2018) demonstrated this through a controlled study: students asked to reduce social media use to 30 minutes daily showed significant declines in loneliness and depression within three weeks. What mattered was not abstinence but awareness. Participants first logged their baseline usage, then adjusted from knowledge rather than impulse. Diagnosis, in this sense, precedes liberation.

Yet awareness alone does not guarantee action. Many professionals run digital audits once, find the results alarming, and then promptly forget them. This is because information without interpretation stalls. A diagnostic process must include a rubric—a structured way to score and compare. One practical method ranks each digital activity on three axes: *utility* (does it help me advance my aims?), *impact* (does it energise or deplete me?), and *frequency* (how often does it recur?). The result is a grid of intention. A tool that is low-utility, high-frequency, and draining is a candidate for redesign. A platform that is high-utility but exhausting may need boundaries, not bans.

The NHS's *Five Ways to Wellbeing* framework (2008) applied similar logic in a non-digital domain: diagnose daily behaviours before prescribing change. The programme asked participants to log acts of "connect, be active, take notice, keep learning, give." The diagnosis revealed neglected domains, enabling targeted micro-shifts. Translating this to digital life means asking: which of my online behaviours connect, which numb, which teach, which take? Such questions require courage precisely because they are empirical, not rhetorical.

Counter-examples remind us why denial persists. Some professions depend on continuous digital engagement—financial traders, emergency coordinators, social media managers. For them, a reductionist "screen-time bad" narrative collapses. The reconciliation lies in *contextual diagnosis*: measure not hours but *alignment with role*. A trader's eight-hour Bloomberg session may be perfectly aligned; a teacher's eight-hour inbox vigil may not. Denial often hides behind role inflation: "It's part of my job." Diagnosis punctures that defence by distinguishing necessary from habitual.

The motif of the *mirror* fits here. Diagnosis holds up a mirror that reflects behaviour without distortion. But mirrors can intimidate. The brain's default stance under cognitive dissonance is avoidance—ignoring data that threatens identity. This is why digital audits must begin with neutrality. The language matters: replace "I wasted" with

"I used." Replace "I should" with "I notice." The goal is description before prescription. The NHS uses this order in clinical diagnostics for a reason: until observation stabilises, intervention destabilises.

Technology firms have begun institutionalising diagnosis at scale. In 2021, *SAP* introduced the *Digital Wellbeing Index*, a self-assessment embedded in its employee portal. Workers rated statements such as "I check messages during family time" or "I can focus without digital distraction" on a five-point scale. Results generated personalised dashboards showing digital strain levels. Participation was voluntary; uptake exceeded 70 per cent. The effect was cultural: conversation replaced denial. Once quantified, distraction could be discussed without stigma.

A parallel can be drawn to athletic performance. Elite cyclists use power meters not to judge themselves but to detect fatigue before failure. The data remove ego from decision. Similarly, a truthful digital inventory prevents emotional overreaction. It separates signal from shame. Once the baseline is known, improvement can be plotted with the calm of engineering, not the drama of repentance.

The diagnostic mindset also reframes *help* and *harm*. Not all engagement is equal. Messaging friends for emotional support differs from doom-scrolling through conflict threads. Yet both may occupy the same category on a screen-time chart. Diagnosis contextualises metrics. It asks not just *how much*, but *to what end*. For example, studies by the Oxford Internet Institute (Przybylski & Weinstein, 2019) found that moderate social media use (up to one hour daily) correlated with higher wellbeing in adolescents, while both extremes—none and excessive—showed declines. The nuance is the lesson: the goal is calibration, not abstinence.

Denial often masquerades as optimism—"I'm managing fine." But real management begins with measurement. When teams conduct collective audits—time studies, meeting counts, notification tallies—they uncover systemic, not personal, inefficiencies. Atlassian's *State of Teams* report (2022) found that employees spent 31 per cent of their week in meetings they deemed unnecessary. Once that figure was named, teams began self-pruning agendas without managerial decrees. Diagnosis created shared agency.

A credible limitation must be faced: diagnosis can slide into self-surveillance. Excessive tracking becomes its own compulsion, converting reflection into control. The reconciliation lies in rhythm. Weekly audits suffice; daily ones may breed anxiety. The point is insight, not inspection. The question to ask is simple: *Does this data help me act with more ease?* If not, discard the metric. A diagnostic tool that tightens the mind has missed the spirit of stillness.

Honest inventory also requires boundaries of evidence. A digital audit should integrate subjective and objective data—how time *felt*, not only how it was logged. A calendar entry saying "emails 9:00–11:00" records time; a note saying "felt scattered after 40 minutes" records cost. The two together form diagnosis. The first quantifies; the second qualifies. One without the other is denial in disguise.

Once gathered, data must lead somewhere. The next stage—Intention—will translate diagnosis into aim. But before that, pause. Because diagnosis is not neutral administration; it is moral clarity in spreadsheet form. It tells the truth about what your attention feeds. The harm of denial is not ignorance—it is misallocation. Every hour misread is a value misplaced. The digital audit, then, is a kind of confession without religion, a practice of seeing one's inputs before judging outputs.

To sustain honesty, the Stillness Protocol recommends a simple heuristic borrowed from clinical practice: *If you can't measure it, describe it; if you can't describe it, question it.* That last clause saves the process from delusion. What resists description often hides the most powerful distortions—doom-scrolling rationalised as research, endless tabs disguised as learning. To name is to limit; to limit is to choose.

The motif of the mirror returns for the final reflection. Mirrors do not flatter or condemn; they reveal. Diagnosis performs that same unglamorous function in the ecology of stillness. It stops us mistaking motion for meaning. Yet even here, an unresolved tension remains: what if the truth revealed is uncomfortable, unfixable, or at odds with one's livelihood? The forward test is simple but demanding—will you still look? The quality of calm that follows depends less on what the data say, and more on whether you have the courage to keep the mirror clean.

Run the Interventions

In April 2017, at the offices of *Basecamp* in Chicago, a small experiment changed how the company worked. The leadership introduced a new rhythm called "The Cycle": six weeks of focused work, two weeks of cool-down. During each cycle, teams chose three specific improvements—small, bounded, measurable. They tracked outcomes, not hours. The gains were startlingly consistent: fewer abandoned projects, higher satisfaction scores, less burnout. The mechanism wasn't mystical. It was disciplined iteration—run the interventions, measure the difference, adjust the design. What began as an internal schedule became a philosophy of compounding focus.

The Stillness Protocol asks for the same method at the level of individual and collective attention. Having diagnosed one's digital life, the next move is execution—*not wholesale reinvention, but calibrated intervention.* The discipline lies in choosing *three* deliberate changes, sustaining them for *two weeks*, and measuring their effect against value metrics you actually care about: clarity, rest, quality of presence. This cycle, repeated, is how momentum builds—slowly, visibly, irreversibly.

Interventions work best when ranked by effort and impact. This simple two-axis rubric, adapted from operations design, prevents self-improvement from collapsing into self-punishment. High-impact, low-effort actions—such as setting "do not disturb" periods or scheduling a single deep-work block—offer immediate return. Low-impact, high-effort changes, like deleting all social media, rarely endure. The art is in selection, not extremity. Small, measurable wins alter the baseline of attention. Like a physicist adjusting initial conditions, we change the trajectory by millimetres, not miles.

Behavioural science validates this modesty. In 2009, BJ Fogg's research at Stanford showed that habit formation succeeds when the change is specific, easy, and emotionally rewarding. The team's "Tiny Habits" framework found that performing a small act (like flossing one tooth or opening a notebook) triggered disproportionately large long-term adoption. The implication is clear: interventions that respect friction outperform those that fight it. The Stillness Protocol borrows this precision—three selected actions, repeated consciously, then reviewed with evidence.

Consider the case of *Deloitte Digital*'s 2020 "Focus Sprint" experiment in its London studio. Teams committed to reducing digital interruptions by instituting three rules for a fortnight: silent channels before 10 a.m., one status update daily, and no after-hours Slack use. Productivity rose 18 per cent, and project rework dropped by 12 per cent. But the deeper outcome was psychological: employees reported feeling "permissioned to focus." This phrase captures the essence of intervention—an act of reclaiming agency through agreed boundaries.

Each intervention should trace back to its diagnostic findings. If your audit shows attention fragmentation, you might trial batching communication or introducing friction before app access. If fatigue dominates, experiment with end-of-day shutdown rituals or deliberate device distance. Each test functions as an empirical micro-lab: modify one variable, observe the consequence. Over time, the feedback loop stabilises behaviour into rhythm. Philosophy becomes cadence.

The motif of *momentum* runs through this process. Momentum, in physics, is mass multiplied by velocity. In behavioural change, it is value multiplied by consistency. The first few cycles of intervention may feel negligible, but their compound effect is exponential. A two-week success becomes confidence; confidence fuels commitment; commitment creates cumulative calm. The system doesn't demand perfection—it rewards persistence. The crucial principle is *continuity over intensity*.

The structure mirrors agile methodology but applies it inwardly. Agile teams iterate in sprints, adjusting to feedback; individuals in the Stillness Protocol iterate through reflection cycles. Both depend on metrics. Without measurement, there is no learning—only repetition. That is why every intervention must include at least one *value metric*. For attention work, the most reliable indicators are qualitative: perceived clarity, emotional reactivity, sleep quality, or sense of completion. Quantitative proxies—screen time, message counts, open tabs—supplement but never replace self-report. A mind's calm cannot be fully digitised; it must be *felt.*

To make progress visible, the protocol recommends a weekly "delta log": a short note documenting what changed and how it felt. Over time, these logs become a ledger of stillness. At *IDEO* in Palo Alto, designers used a similar technique during their 2018 "Resilience by Design" project, tracking stress markers and work satisfaction through brief daily reflections. Participants reported that simply *writing* the metric improved self-regulation. Observation, once structured, becomes intervention itself.

There are, of course, risks. Some people turn interventions into moral crusades—counting every notification silenced as virtue, every relapse as failure. That distortion replaces curiosity with control. The countermeasure is humility: treating each cycle as an experiment, not a verdict. The point is not to purify behaviour but to *understand its mechanics.* A failed intervention still yields data; it reveals boundary conditions. Progress is not linear, but it is cumulative.

Consider a contrasting example: *Microsoft Japan*'s "Work-Life Choice Challenge" (August 2019), where a company-wide four-day week increased productivity by 40 per cent. The success inspired other divisions to copy the format—only to find morale collapse months later. The reason? They replicated the form without maintaining feedback loops. When interventions become slogans, they die. The Stillness Protocol insists on shorter cycles and ongoing review precisely to prevent ossification. Stillness, paradoxically, survives by moving.

A useful motif here is *iteration as kindness.* Iteration is forgiving by design; it assumes error and welcomes correction. Instead of moralising behaviour, it mechanises learning. Each two-week cycle invites the practitioner to run a humane experiment on themselves: What if I mute my phone after 8 p.m.? What if I start the day with pen and paper instead of a feed? The results are immediate yet subtle—less cortisol, clearer recall, more creative drift. The reward is not heroism but relief.

Empirical studies confirm the benefit of cyclic experimentation. In *Organizational Behaviour and Human Decision Processes* (2015), Ethan Burris and colleagues found that iterative goal-setting outperformed static targets in sustaining motivation across six months. Participants who reviewed and adjusted goals fortnightly maintained higher engagement and satisfaction. The logic applies perfectly to stillness work: change only what you can measure within your control window, then reassess. The rhythm of reflection builds resilience.

To maintain psychological realism, interventions must also acknowledge constraint. Not every improvement is feasible in every life phase. A parent with small children or a surgeon on rotation cannot simply block hours of silence. For them, interventions must adapt to available bandwidth—perhaps a ten-minute device sabbath or a commute debrief. The rubric remains: effort low, impact real. Stillness is scalable, not fragile.

Momentum compounds further when shared. Teams that align on interventions—like a group choosing common quiet hours or conducting joint digital audits—generate social proof. Collective adherence lowers individual friction. The *Behavioural Insights Team* in the UK demonstrated this effect in 2014 when departments synchronised "focus hours." Compliance exceeded 80 per cent once policies were shared publicly. As in finance, compound interest works faster in groups.

But there is a limit. Over-structuring interventions can sterilise the spirit of stillness. If every minute becomes a metric, spontaneity dies. The balance lies in alternating rigour with grace—structure guiding awareness, not suffocating it. The Stillness Protocol's weekly rehearsal guards this balance. It embeds discipline within compassion, measurement within meaning.

The quiet motif of *momentum* closes the circle. Momentum, once established, has its own ethics: it resists collapse. Yet sustaining it requires vigilance against drift—against the complacency of assuming that calm, once gained, will persist without maintenance. The forward test is simple: which three interventions, if run now, would improve not productivity but *presence*? That question defines the next cycle.

The experiment begins again. Three choices. Two weeks. One metric that matters. Measure, adjust, repeat. The gains are small, then compound, then structural—until stillness stops being something you practise and becomes the way your system breathes.

Keep the Charter Alive

In Toyota City, Aichi Prefecture, the early practitioners of *hoshin kanri* instituted monthly *obeya* reviews—wall-to-wall rooms where managers and line leaders stood together to revisit the plan (Toyota, 1960s onward). Charts were not trophies but tools. Assumptions were annotated in red. Actions were re-assigned in public. If a target had slipped, the question was not *who failed?* but *what did the system miss?* The ritual mattered more than the metrics. By meeting the plan every month, they kept it from ossifying. The charter lived because it was amended. Amendments keep documents honest.

A stillness charter deserves the same governance. It is not a manifesto to frame; it is a compact to maintain—updated at a cadence, tested against evidence, and strengthened through accountability. Left untouched, even the best charter calcifies into decor. Signatures fade. Habits drift. The world shifts under the document's feet. A monthly review arrests that entropy. It restores relation between text and life. The motif for this subchapter is the *margin*: the white space where living documents acquire small, precise edits that change how the whole page reads.

Show → Name → Explain → Implication. Show: on the first Friday of each month, you open last month's charter and your attention ledger side by side. *Name:* charter review. *Explain:* you scan five items: purpose, non-purpose, red lines, defaults, and experiments. For each, you ask: *What did the data say? Where did friction rise? Where did ease appear? Implication:* the charter adapts rather than accuses. It rewards reality. The act is administrative in form but moral in effect. You commit again, but you commit accurately.

Iteration without external witness risks drift. Hence *accountability partners.* In Alcoholics Anonymous, founded in Akron, Ohio, in 1935, the sponsor—someone a few steps further along—anchors the newcomer's practice through regular check-ins. Sponsorship works because it joins confession to craft: you report to someone who recognises the patterns and the pitfalls. Translate that logic to stillness: share your charter with one colleague or friend and schedule a 20-minute monthly exchange. The conversation is structured: What was promised? What was measured? What is now amended? This is not surveillance; it is stewardship. Being seen keeps the margin honest.

Two named, checkable examples illustrate how live documents become culture. First, Toyota's *hoshin* cycles in the 1960s–70s formalised monthly catch-ball: goals moving up and down the hierarchy until they fit reality. The *obeya* room turned abstraction into conversation; the margin belonged to everyone. Second, Google's OKR process—imported from Intel's Andy Grove (1970s, Santa Clara) and publicised at Google from 1999 onwards—works when teams hold regular check-ins to grade and revise objectives. Quarterly targets are famous; the less famous monthly reviews are where the learning happens. In both cases, the metric is a means. The meeting is the machinery.

A credible limitation belongs on the page. Some charters collapse under *too much* revision. A team that edits weekly may signal indecision; an individual who moves the red lines monthly may be gaming the game. Reconciliation sits in the cadence. Monthly is generous enough to collect evidence and scarce enough to preserve stability. Urgent exceptions are possible—real life insists on them—but they are marked as exceptions, not defaults. The margin records the reason. Over time, the document tells a story that can be audited: *we changed this because*… The because matters.

The charter's vitality depends on evidence. Talk is cheap; measurement is not. Pair every clause with a behaviour, metric, or decision. If the charter says *silent phone before bed*, track sleep onset time and subjective morning clarity. If it says *calendar-first work*, count context switches and completed deep blocks. If it says *batch communications*, tally messages sent and "oops, ignore previous" corrections. The point is not to become a spreadsheet. It is to let numbers temper narrative so the margin carries weight. Evidence dignifies amendment.

Accountability does not mean spectacle. Public performativity warps intentions. Choose a small circle—two peers, a partner, a trusted mentor—and share the charter privately. The theatre of virtue corrodes practice; visibility should serve vigilance, not vanity. Sociologist Erving Goffman noted how front-stage behaviour distorts self-presentation. Your charter belongs backstage. The front-stage change is quieter: emails that read cleaner; meetings that end on time; evenings that no longer fray.

Evidence precedes teaching, but teaching completes the loop. Transmission stabilises practice. In 1950, W. Edwards Deming taught post-war Japanese executives the Plan-Do-Study-Act cycle; its genius was not just statistical control but a pedagogy: learn it, run it, then teach it to someone else. Teaching converts tacit skill into explicit grammar; it compels you to clarify methods you had been half-guessing. When you walk a colleague through your charter—why a red line is a red line, how you run reviews—you discover holes you had politely ignored. The margin thickens with better ink.

The charter gains authority by absorbing failure without melodrama. A month with missed marks is a gift if it yields clean revision. Consider the NHS's "Learning from Deaths" process (England, 2017): trusts review selected cases monthly, with a structured tool to pull lessons into governance. The model is sober and humane: error is treated as teacher, not tormentor. Stillness charters deserve the same tone. If your digital sabbath failed three Saturdays in a row, write the reason in the margin and shrink the claim: *reactivity-free mornings*, not *no screens*. Let reality coach the vow.

Ritual anchors review. Choose a time and make it felt. Some teams light the same lamp, play the same 30-second chime, and open the same two windows: charter and ledger. Small sensory cues hasten arrival. Microsoft's Human Factors Lab has shown that even brief pauses between meetings drop stress markers; the same logic applies here. A minute of silence before amendment restores judgment. You will cut truer lines when the nervous system is level. Calm edits better than adrenaline.

The charter's architecture benefits from provenance. Date every amendment. Note authorship when shared. The paper trail builds trust, especially in teams. Over months, a living document becomes a map of collective learning: *we adopted scheduled send in March; we added "attention roles" in June; we dropped Friday stand-ups in September.* Artefacts like this survive personnel changes; they teach newcomers—without shaming—how attention is protected here. Culture is partly what a group refuses to forget. The charter trains memory.

Teaching outward strengthens inward. The parent who explains a device clause to a teenager must hold it up to questions; the manager who onboards a new hire into the team's humane defaults must translate values into operations. In both, the act of explanation converts habit into doctrine into habit again. The transmission should include *why*, not just *what*: *We pin apologies because repair must be findable. We end meetings with reflection because memory is formed at the edge.* Shared rationale survives pressure better than shared rules.

There is a further ethical dividend. Monthly reviews with an accountability partner diversify attention. Another person's questions reveal your blind spots. "You say right speech matters; why does your subject-line contract still bury the verb?" "You value presence at home; why is your watch vibrating at dinner?" These are not gotchas. They are mirrors. Good partners ask for receipts. The charter grows up under that gaze.

Beware the counter-movement: review theatre. Some organisations ritualise check-ins while quietly rewarding the opposite behaviour. They publish charters, then promote people who never pause. The remedy is alignment. Ensure that incentives match clauses: performance criteria must include attention quality, not just throughput. A charter without teeth becomes literature. A charter with incentives becomes law. Law, here, is kinder than posture; it protects the vulnerable against the loud.

Language shapes longevity. Write charters in plain Anglo-Saxon where possible—short verbs, concrete nouns. Replace "optimise" with "shorten Mondays' meetings by 20 minutes." Replace "enhance focus" with "two hours' single-thread block daily." Edits in the margin should tighten semantics. Precision endures storms. Ambiguity frays at the first gust.

Metrics, again, are ballast. Choose a few that mean something locally. In families: device-free dinners per week; bedtime stability; bedtime mood. In research groups: deep-block counts; revision loops avoided; decision latency after meeting reforms. In clinics: patient complaint rates about brusqueness on Mondays; handover errors after weekends. The charter ties numbers to nouns. The nouns, in turn, keep numbers humane.

Transmission has a civic face. Departments that publish short, clear charters—one page, four quadrants, last amended date—invite dialogue rather than decree. Public service bodies do this with "service standards"; universities do it with "assessment briefs." Your context can do it with *attention standards*: the rules by which you protect thought. When these standards travel—between teams, professions, homes—they stabilise practice beyond personality. That is how stillness becomes a local norm rather than a private eccentricity.

Return to the *margin*. Each amendment is small. Yet, over a year, small edits change a life. The monthly ritual teaches a lesson that Toyota, Deming, and recovery communities share: constancy of review breeds constancy of behaviour. You do not become rigid. You become reliable. The charter, kept alive, becomes less like an aspiration and more like an operating system—quiet, dependable, and tuned to reality.

An unresolved test remains, and it belongs to you. When the next month turns, which one clause of your charter most deserves a line in the margin—and whose eyes, other than yours, will read it before it takes effect? If you cannot name the clause or the witness, the document is sleeping. Wake it. Then teach one person why you changed it. Transmission will finish what intention started.

Chapter 9
Grace After the Feed (Epilogue of Use)

In March 2020, as hospitals across northern Italy filled beyond capacity, a nurse in Bergamo named Chiara began leaving her phone on the ward windowsill during each twelve-hour shift. The beeping never stopped—alerts, calls, messages from home—but she had learned that the only way to preserve her humanity was to choose her silences. "Discipline kept me functioning," she later said, "but compassion kept me human." When she walked out each evening, she didn't check her feed; she texted a single colleague instead: *Still here?* The reply, often delayed but almost always returned, became their ritual of grace. The device was the same; the use had changed. Technology hadn't disappeared—it had been domesticated by tenderness.

We often think mastery over the digital depends on control: the strict routine, the clean inbox, the perfect attention span. But control alone cannot carry us through the human mess of relapse. The feed always returns, the dopamine curve resets, the scroll resumes. What distinguishes the resilient from the rigid is *how they recover.* This closing chapter begins where discipline ends—with grace. If earlier sections of this book have mapped structure, this one asks what sustains it when the structure cracks. It argues that compassion is not indulgence; it is maintenance. It is the antifragile glue that lets practice survive failure.

Across a nurse's ward, a coder's workspace, and a parent's home, the same truth repeats: perfection collapses under pressure, but kindness bends and rebounds. The nurse in Bergamo measured mercy in moments; the coder in Bangalore learned it in code reviews; the parent in Manchester practised it at the dinner table, resisting the reflex to multitask through bedtime stories. Each learned that digital discipline without emotional literacy breeds brittleness. The Stillness Protocol—the architecture of diagnosis, design, and practice—demands a final ingredient: gentleness toward the self that falters.

To understand why, we must trace how discipline alone fails. In behavioural economics, the "ego depletion" hypothesis once claimed that self-control is a finite resource. Though later contested, its core metaphor remains useful: effort exhausts. Every digital abstinence—every ignored notification or resisted scroll—draws on mental credit. Over time, that account runs low. Without renewal through compassion, the deficit breeds guilt, then resignation. A system designed for stillness becomes one more arena for self-reproach. Grace interrupts that spiral. It reframes relapse not as evidence of weakness but as feedback about limits.

The coder's story illustrates this with precision. In 2022, Raghav, a software engineer for a health-tech start-up in Bengaluru, began logging "micro-lapses"—moments when he broke his own deep-work rules. At first, he punished himself with stricter schedules. Productivity rose, but mood declined. His turning point came after reading the *postmortem* culture of Site Reliability Engineering at Google—where failures are dissected without blame. Raghav adopted the same tone with himself: each lapse became a data point, not a moral flaw. Within weeks, his code reviews improved. "I started debugging my habits the way I debugged software," he said. That shift—from shame to curiosity—is the birth of compassion in digital practice.

Grace, in this context, is not softness; it is structural intelligence. It turns setbacks into scaffolds. A compassionate stance allows systems to flex under load. In Nassim Taleb's terms, it is *antifragility*: systems that improve through stress. The parent in Manchester exemplified this when she discovered her household's "tech-free dinners" were collapsing under teenage protest. Instead of scrapping the rule, she amended it: thirty minutes of shared silence, then five minutes of collective scrolling to share memes or stories. The family ritual survived because it evolved. Compassion didn't lower the bar; it kept the habit alive.

This closing chapter synthesises the tools introduced throughout the book—the audits, charters, interventions, and reviews—into a single stance: *gentle authority*. The goal is neither abstinence nor indulgence but stewardship. To rule one's attention is not to banish tools but to re-establish hierarchy: human first, device second. Compassion ensures that hierarchy remains humane. It reminds us that every rule must serve life, not the reverse.

Philosophically, this is not new. In the fourth century, the Desert Fathers—Christian ascetics living in the Egyptian wilderness—kept simple rules for daily discipline. Yet their most radical teaching was forgiveness: when a monk broke his fast or fell asleep in prayer, others would say, "He is tired from the struggle." The point was not to excuse failure but to preserve continuity of devotion. The same logic applies to our digital vows. When we lapse, we are not lost; we are simply tired from the struggle. Compassion restores the will to try again.

In organisational science, the same principle underpins what Harvard's Amy Edmondson calls *psychological safety*: environments where error is not weaponised but examined. Teams with higher psychological safety outperform because they recover faster. The parallel in digital life is exact: the compassionate practitioner iterates; the punitive one quits. Compassion doesn't dilute accountability—it deepens it by removing fear.

The motif of *grace* threads quietly through this chapter. Grace is the pause between notification and reaction; the breath before reply; the decision to ask, *What does this moment need?* rather than *What do I need to control?* It is the state that allows stillness to remain human-scaled. Without it, discipline decays into dogma. With it, practice becomes culture.

The chapter unfolds through three intertwined narratives—a nurse who learns to anchor presence amid chaos, a coder who replaces self-censure with curiosity, and a parent who rebuilds attention as a family value. Their stories converge on one idea: that mastery over tools must mature into mercy within their use. Together they demonstrate that the endpoint of stillness is not austerity but affection—for our devices, for our minds, for one another.

Grace, then, is not the opposite of rigour; it is its fulfilment. To be kind toward distraction is not to surrender to it but to understand its roots. It is the stance of one who knows that discipline starts movements but compassion sustains them. The Stillness Protocol was always meant to culminate here—in a practice that can forgive itself.

The pages ahead invite the reader to explore this final synthesis: how to hold capability tethered to kindness, and how to exercise authority without cruelty. It is a fitting epilogue for an age defined by feeds and fatigue. Discipline made us attentive; compassion will make us whole. The feed ends, but grace remains.

Why Compassion Finishes What Discipline Starts

In April 2020, when Lombardy was the epicentre of Europe's COVID-19 crisis, a nurse named Chiara Bianchi spent twenty-one consecutive days on shift in Bergamo's Papa Giovanni XXIII Hospital. Between ventilators and video calls to dying patients' families, she noticed something quietly radical in the ward's rhythm. The nurses stopped reprimanding each other for errors born of exhaustion; instead, they shared corrections in whispers, ending with, "Rest when you can." Later, when asked how she kept her team from fracturing, Bianchi said: "Discipline got us through the first week. Compassion got us through the rest." Her phrase captures a profound truth about the human condition under technological and temporal pressure: strictness can start reform, but only tenderness sustains it.

Digital self-mastery—this book's terrain—often begins in rigour. We track screen time, schedule sabbaths, craft charters. Yet each measure eventually collides with fatigue, temptation, or relapse. The problem is not weakness but biology. The prefrontal cortex, seat of restraint, tires faster than the limbic system's craving for novelty. Without grace, the inevitable lapse becomes self-sabotage. Compassion, correctly understood, is not leniency. It is antifragility: the capacity to grow stronger through stress. Where discipline carves a channel, compassion keeps it from cracking.

A coder in Bengaluru named Raghav learned this the hard way. In 2022, while leading a product sprint for a telemedicine start-up, he set a personal rule—no Slack between 9 a.m. and noon. For three days, it held. On the fourth, a client emergency shattered his resolve.

That night, ashamed, he rebuilt his blocklists and vowed to "try harder." Within a week, the pattern repeated. The turning point came when his manager showed him Google's internal "postmortem" reports, which analyse failures without blame. Borrowing that model, Raghav began running postmortems on himself: every lapse was logged, discussed, and redesigned. The data was humbling—his "failures" clustered on days after late-night debugging. Once he added an earlier cut-off for evening work, interruptions dropped by half. "I stopped treating myself as a sinner," he said, "and started treating myself as a system." Compassion, here, functioned as operational intelligence.

Compassion's power lies in its paradox: it looks soft but acts as structure. A parent in Manchester discovered this after months of enforcing "no-phones-at-dinner" with her teenage sons. The rule provoked more resentment than reflection. Finally, she changed it—thirty minutes of device-free eating followed by five minutes of "feed-sharing," where each person showed one thing they had saved that week. The tension dissolved. What began as prohibition became exchange. Compassion converted defiance into participation. By loosening the grip, she preserved the value.

The motif threading through these lives is *repair*. Repair assumes breakage. A life governed by screens will always fracture around its ideals. The purpose of compassion is not to erase those cracks but to make them generative. Psychological studies affirm this principle. Kristin Neff's 2011 research on self-compassion found that individuals who treated personal failures with kindness were more likely to resume difficult habits—exercise, diet, or mindfulness—than those who responded with guilt. The reason is neurological: shame activates the threat system; compassion activates the caregiving system, restoring equilibrium. In other words, forgiveness fuels persistence.

Contrast this with cultures that sanctify discipline alone. Silicon Valley's "grind ethos," crystallised in the mantra *move fast and break things*, rewards intensity but punishes reflection. When burnout ensues, workers leave, and companies restart the cycle with fresh recruits. The result is momentum without maturity. The limitation of pure rigour is fragility—it cannot tolerate variance. The antifragile system, by contrast, anticipates error and metabolises it. Compassion is that metabolism.

History offers precedent. In the fourth century, the Desert Fathers—Christian monks living in Egypt's Scetis Valley—devised elaborate rules for ascetic life. Yet the senior monk, Abba Poemen, taught: "A man may fall a thousand times and still rise, if he says, 'I will begin again.'" Their genius was procedural forgiveness: lapses weren't moral failures but iterations. Each return deepened the discipline. This is the lineage modern attention practice must reclaim—not of harsh renunciation, but of iterative fidelity.

To synthesise the tools introduced earlier—audits, charters, interventions, reviews—compassion must become their atmosphere. Without it, the system hardens into a spreadsheet of guilt. With it, each tool becomes responsive, alive to context. A digital audit, run with curiosity rather than condemnation, reveals design flaws instead of moral ones. An accountability partner, approached as ally not warden, invites candour. The monthly charter review, infused with forgiveness, becomes not judgment day but calibration. Compassion finishes what discipline starts because it converts protocol into culture.

Empirically, this transition resembles what organisational psychologists call *psychological safety*. Amy Edmondson's research at Harvard Business School (1999) showed that medical teams who admitted more errors were, paradoxically, safer than those reporting fewer. The difference was not competence but candour. Teams that felt secure to disclose mistakes learned faster. Compassion thus scales: from self to system, from habit to institution. When individuals permit their own lapses, they model it for others. Over time, this builds environments where attention is protected not by fear of failure but by shared humility.

The nurse, the coder, and the parent demonstrate three levels of this ecology. The nurse embodies compassion under crisis—presence amid overload. The coder exemplifies compassion through analysis—curiosity replacing shame. The parent shows compassion in relationship—boundaries animated by warmth. Together, they form a triad of modern virtue: endurance, intelligence, and empathy.

Their stories reveal that the ultimate maturity of digital life is not austerity but *gentle authority*.

Gentle authority differs from permissiveness. It sets limits but does so with grace. A person practising gentle authority does not discard the phone; they domesticate it. They know when to silence it, when to listen, when to let it ring. In leadership terms, it mirrors the shift from command-and-control to servant leadership—a model in which power protects rather than polices. Within the digital sphere, this means designing systems that respect recovery: user interfaces that end rather than extend attention, workplaces that celebrate deep rest as productivity, families that honour pauses as connection.

There are limits. Compassion can be weaponised as avoidance—the corporate wellness initiative that preaches self-care while doubling workloads; the parent who confuses indulgence for empathy. Genuine compassion demands discernment. It recognises suffering without collapsing into sentimentality. To finish what discipline starts, it must remain anchored in evidence—measurable behaviours, trackable outcomes, visible relief. In practice, that means noticing whether a policy actually reduces anxiety, whether a ritual genuinely restores attention. Compassion earns its name through effect, not expression.

A useful metaphor returns us to Chiara's ward in Bergamo. Each night, before leaving, she washed her hands twice—once for hygiene, once for closure. The second wash, she said, was "for what couldn't be fixed." That gesture, unrecorded in any manual, carried the essence of this chapter. It acknowledged imperfection while marking intent to continue. Compassion, like that wash, cleans nothing but clarifies everything.

The motif of *repair* closes here as it began. Every digital discipline—every focus protocol, audit, or ritual—will fracture. The test of maturity is whether we respond with fury or forgiveness. Compassion is not a postscript to discipline; it is its evolution. The final lesson of the Stillness Protocol, then, is not abstinence from technology but allegiance to humanity. Tools need not diminish us if we meet them with gentler authority—rules guided by empathy, capability tethered to kindness.

The forward question lingers: when the next lapse arrives—as it surely will—will you choose to patch the crack with punishment or with care? The answer will decide not just how you use your tools, but how you inhabit your attention.

About the Author

Raised between prayer mats and command lines, Fatima al-Karim writes at the seam where contemplative traditions meet the restless glow of modern screens. Her work treats attention as both a craft and a conscience, drawing on the quiet grammar of dhikr, the Buddhist art of returning, and the ordinary mercies of daily life. She has led community workshops on humane technology, helped families draft "stillness charters," and spends long winter walks testing which rituals survive cold and Wi-Fi. Fatima's pages favour clarity over grand claims: small, durable practices; ethics that travel; language that breathes. She believes the question is not whether to abandon our tools but how to carry them without becoming their carriers—an old pilgrim's problem with new notifications. When she is not writing, she is making soup, answering slowly, and stitching silence back into the day.

www.ingramcontent.com/pod-product-compliance
Lightning Source LLC
Chambersburg PA
CBHW031345230926
51848CB00002B/397